Pieces
in
her **Mind**

An Autobiography

Pamela Combs

iUniverse, Inc.
New York   Bloomington

Pieces in Her Mind

iUniverse books may be ordered through booksellers or by contacting:

iUniverse
1663 Liberty Drive
Bloomington, IN 47403
www.iuniverse.com
1-800-Authors (1-800-288-4677)

ISBN: 978-1-4401-1775-6 (pbk)
ISBN: 978-1-4401-1954-5 (ebk)

Printed in the United States of America

iUniverse rev. date: 1/15/2009

Our Son

Look! He's a boy
So proudly announced
Overjoyed with pride

Contempt was so far away
A race to win his love
Puppy dog tails

The color light blue
Courage was a word of the past
Love is a word for the future

"Gallantly," said his father
"Wish," said his mother
All came true.

Pamela Combs

Author's Notes

Some of the names and places in this autobiography have been changed in order to maintain the dignity and privacy of others. It discusses a person's life that is mentally ill.

This autobiography depicts language that is developed from a mentally ill person's viewpoint. The vocabulary and dialect are from a person that is from the hills of Kentucky.

This autobiography is based on a person's mentally ill life from the ages two to fifty. The book clearly shows how one person fell from success after becoming mentally ill. It shows how that person struggles to regain hope.

Prologue

The water was almost oblivious to the hands that swished through its soapy content. The gazing memory of the past crept through as the water rippled through hands that became farther, farther…away. He walked through the grass as if to give her a glimpse of his shirt that he wore that morning. His hair was slightly curled around the nape of his sweaty neck. Suddenly Pam's thoughts became reality as did the scalding water in the sink. Her mind was at a loss to what she'd actually just seen. It was the beginning of a long journey through time that will last nine to eleven years. The memories jumbled together as if never to be forgotten or to come to an end.

Harold was gone with his buddies golfing. He thought of his wife and his son. He would mention Wade to his friend every now and then but rarely spoke of his thirty-eight year old wife. She'd been doing some things that weren't really in her character to do. She kept him awake to all hours of the night, getting up and down from the bed. "How could she not sleep?" he thought as she taught school all day and came home to a house ready for laundry and dinner. This has gone on for weeks on end. Harold's friend asked "Hey are you okay?" He just replied, "I'm a little tired, but I'll be fine once I get a full night's sleep."

Pam knew it was near time for Harold to come home from his golfing trip. What she actually thought she saw scared her. She began to run through the house yelling, "Wade where are you?" Her seven year old son had a long day at kindergarten. He was laying on the couch in the basement while Power Rangers fought fearlessly on the television. With the remote in her hand she lowered the volume. She studied her son's face. His eyes were unseen under the purplish lids and row of black eyelashes. His mouth was slightly open as he breathed in and out softly. Her love for him and her husband brought tears to her eyes. But the unsettling nights had taken its toll on Pam too. She sank to the floor and curled against the carpet's rough texture as it engulfed her body she fell into a deep sleep that would last until nightfall.

Pam thought of this episode and wondered why that was the beginning of her journey into a lost world of hope. Her fingers trembled as she jotted these things down on paper. Then she was interrupted by her caretaker at Lexington's Grassy Personal Care Home as they told her Wade and Harold were there for a visit. It felt good to see her eighteen year old son again. She laughed when she saw them standing in the hallway. They'd all been going through these meetings for a long time. Time had chipped away at their familiarity with each other.

Pam wasn't your everyday KERA teacher. She had gone from a successful teaching career of rewards to a world that unfolded into a world of sickness.

Chapter 1

Pam was awakened by her dream. Harold was sleeping beside her. The sheets and quilt on the bed seemed to bog and twist around her body as if they wanted to strangle her. She twisted and turned as quietly as she could to be free of them. The hardwood floor was cool and slick beneath Pam's feet as she made her way down the dark stairway to a corner in the basement. Sitting in a squatting position with the gown pulled over her knees, Pam began to go over her events that day. The strange people walking past her door at school had brought tears to her face as she wrote on the chalkboard. Why were they staring at her as they walked past her door? The amount of traffic on the little gravel road next to her schoolroom window aggravated her to the point of covering her windows by pulling the shades. The sound of the motorcycle seemed to rip through the classroom. As Pam looked at the faces of her students, they seemed engrossed with their writing and didn't notice the sounds and noises of the outside world. Well, she noticed it. Pam wanted to leave the room and pick up her son and go home, but the clock wouldn't let her. It was only time to end the writing assignment and tie it in with the science project they had worked on the day before. Harold's still sleeping as her thoughts rambled on and on. She reached for a cigarette and an ashtray to ease the pain. Before too long the hours just seemed to vanish away. It was time to awaken and go back to the room at school. Pam had done this for weeks on end. How could she continue to have racing thoughts

1

and sleepless nights in the cool basement of their home? Her thoughts were interrupted by her sister's husband, Herman, who was knocking at her door. He pounded until Pam swung the door open wanting to know what he wanted at this time of morning. Both his two daughters were with him but there was no sign of her sister Rita. "I thought you would never answer the door", Herman said. Pam told him she was asleep and asked what was wrong. Herman said that Rita had been missing since Erica, her niece, returned from school. He wanted her to take care of the two girls until he and the rescue party could look for Rita in the woods. Startled by what she had learned, Pam asked, "Is Rita lost in the woods?" Herman didn't know but he said Mary, the other daughter, was home alone when he returned home from work. All the racing thoughts that were running through Pam's head left her. She let the trembling crying girls into her basement and made her way up the stairs to tell Harold and Wade. Herman left to search for Rita. Pam later found out Herman went to his sister's house instead of searching for Rita. The rescue team found Rita on the front porch of her neighbor's house the next morning. Harold took a day off from work to take Rita to the hospital while Pam stayed with the two girls.

Rita had scratches and bruises on her legs where she had stumbled through the woods all night. When Harold arrived, he saw that Rita's legs were bleeding. "Rita, your legs are hurt. Would you like to go to the hospital?" Rita told him that she would, and he drove her to the Berea hospital. All the way there Harold wondered what Herman was doing to Rita and the two girls. Harold was startled when the rescue team called him and asked if he could take Rita to the hospital. Rita wouldn't agree at first but went after he talked with her for a while. After Rita was taken to the hospital the doctor came to the waiting room and asked Harold questions.

As Pam walked through the door, Harold was there to meet them. He worried the girls were sick. Wade explained to his daddy they were happy instead of sad. Harold told all of them that Rita was in good hands and would be home in a few days. When Pam and Harold were alone, she asked him if there was any word from Herman. Harold said he had not heard from him or seen him. Deep down Pam was worried that Herman had somehow abused Rita and the girls or this would not have happened. Pam finally broke down and called Jenny her sister.

Jenny was a tall cool blonde who was a CPA. She worked in different areas in the country and stayed very busy but she always made time for her family. She was especially fond of Wade. Wade and her son Jason were only a year apart in age, and remained close friends from childhood.

Three weeks went by before Rita returned home. In the meantime Herman and his sister picked up his children. They were his. Pam had to let them go. The doctor said they were fine, didn't he? Rita didn't return to her home. She returned to Pam's home. While she was there she told Pam she had been under much pressure raising the girls on the creek. Pam understood and asked if Rita would like to stay with them until she felt secure enough to live on her own. Rita agreed to do this. On a Monday Herman brought Rita's clothes and threw them on the porch. He said she could visit the girls as he saw fit. He had filed for divorce.

Chapter 2

Pam lay in the bed dreading the following day at school. She knew it would be a long day because of the meeting at Wright's Clinic was later that evening. She was secretary of the board and she would need to sign a grant approved by the government for the following year. Pam hoped she would make the right decisions and the clinic would be successful. She knew Wright's Clinic was an important part of the community. It was founded by Dr. Eric Wright years before when Pam was still in high school. Many of the people depended on the clinic for their health care. Jackson County was a small remote place miles away from civilization; it had a few restaurants, two gas stations, and only two dollar stores. The clinic had been under fire by some people in the community for several years. Pam wanted the clinic to do well. She and Wade made frequent visits themselves because of allergies and viruses over the years.

Hours of lying in bed unable to sleep made Pam restless. The quilt seemed to bind and choke her legs. Harold lay on his right side, facing her, almost the whole night. His warm breath seemed to settle her, but her legs were restless and she couldn't stop the thoughts running through her head. It was the Wright's Clinic over and over in her head. It reminded her of the pressure that comes with signing a grant, especially when people's health and lives were in the hands of others. Pam fought back the tears while she dragged herself out of bed. As she walked into her son's room the darkness engulfed her. The wall was bumpy and hot under her fingertips. She touched his foot only to find him still and resting in the dark room of silence. She made her way into the kitchen only to see that the clock said three o'clock. Her corner in the basement was waiting, and she knew this as she found her way down the deep dark staircase. Thoughts of school and the clinic seemed far away as she thought of her mother Sandra. Sandra had lived a life of torment with her mental illness. Pam's sleepless nights had turned into an illness too, but her corner seemed to relieve her from the racing thoughts and dread of the approaching day. Soon it would be time to shower and prepare for the next day. It was cold outside but warm, cozy, and dark in her corner. Little did she know what the following day would be like?

Pam sat that evening as the snow covered ground awaited the melted snow to wet it with its coolness from the night before. She watched television in her basement as Wade played Nintendo in his room. The television seemed to talk to her as she watched the evening news. Things that applied to something she knew about were on the right side of the screen. This went on for hours. It suddenly occurred to her that she was in her pajamas. She had gotten ready for bed. It was seven p.m. It was time for the board meeting at Wright's Clinic. She had signed a grant the month before asking for monies to help the clinic complete their ambitions. She sank onto the floor and began to weep. She was failing at school, and now she was failing at the clinic. Things slowed down to a halt for a couple hours.

Harold came home from his basketball game at school around nine p.m. only to find Pam in the floor of the basement. She was so still. Wade was upstairs asleep in their bed. He had made a habit of crawling into their bed. He slept between them as if he were a cub nuzzling with parents to be safe and serene. Harold wondered if Pam had interacted with Wade at all that evening. But he thought of dinner and lessons she had gone over with Wade at school. He knew she'd worn him down earlier that day. He probably was tired from his play and lessons. Harold didn't think it was a good idea for Wade to be in Pam's classroom, but his preceding teacher recommended it and they went along. Harold scurried back downstairs to find Pam standing next to the television. She was engrossed in something they were saying. Pam seemed not to notice him there. He stammered as he asked her what was going on. Pam seemed preoccupied as she said "I need to get out of the house for a little while." He told her to go ahead.

Pam reached for her keys and wondered what awaited her outside. She took an old bottle of sleeping pills out of the cabinet to take with her. She told Harold she was going for a drive and would be back later. Her lips touched his salty ones as she hurried toward the door. He was wet all over from the basketball game. She climbed into the black Chevy Blazer thinking the traffic was picking up as she left the house. As Pam drove out of the driveway, she took her fingers and found the bottle of sleeping pills in her coat pocket. Down went one, down went two, down went three, then went down some more. The bottle was still half full when she dropped them to the floor. Pam noticed a line of traffic in front of her. She was driving north toward Richmond, Kentucky. The straight stretch of road gave her perfect opportunity to pass the cars ahead. The gas pedal seemed hard to push in as she began to ascend on the row of red tail gate lights. Her Blazer registered sixty, then sixty-eight then seventy before she could see her way clear of the long line of cars. The headlights from the row of cars seemed distant but glared as she told herself to pull off. She continued with the madness, yet soon became bored with her thoughts. She sped off into the darkness more alone than she'd ever been in her life. Where was her staircase and son? Where was the safety of her home, she thought, as she approached a big hill? The pills seemed to slow her down, but she was still having racing thoughts of dieing and why she did what she did. The vehicle began to slow down as she came to the bottom of the hill. Just past the hill there was a country road off to the right of her. Pam decided to drive out the road slowly and find a place to pull off. She drove for what seemed like miles. It was hard to find a place to pull over that wasn't glaring with lights from houses that she passed. Just around the curve Pam felt the Blazer turn around as it flew up over an embankment beside of her. The vehicle was now facing the way in which she'd come, but was sitting on a flat grassy surface. The road down next to her was about four of five feet away. It wasn't level with the surface she was sitting on. Pam sat there for what seemed like hours, but it was only minutes before a white station wagon slowed down to look at her in the Blazer. It was slowing down for the curve, not her. The station wagon had come from behind her, not in front of her. Her Blazer wasn't still running, so she turned the key and the motor began to purr. She slowly turned the wheel of the Blazer while sliding down a small embankment facing the curve she so haphazardly tried to drive around. Slowly she drove back to the main road and turned left to drive home. Pam had never wrecked a vehicle in her life or had a ticket from the police. She'd always driven safely and slowly. She couldn't have been gone from home no longer than thirty or forty minutes before she began her trip back. As Pam pulled into her driveway of her home, she realized she was lucky that the pills weren't taking effect and she had survived what could have been a fatal accident. As she entered the doorway, Harold was sitting in his chair asleep. She thought he seemed pleasant sitting in his chair. She would not tell him of the events she had encountered as she drove out into the dark night. She was glad the racing thoughts and row of traffic had stopped causing her to be agitated. Harold awoke and asked, "Did you have a comforting drive?" She responded with a yes and that she was becoming tired and wanted to go to sleep. So he kissed her unyielding lips and told her good night. Pam saw Wade lying on her side of the bed. Instead of waking him she crawled in beside him on his right side. As she mumbled her prayer she felt a quickening come over her entire body. She said to herself, " I can't die here next to Wade," so she made her way to the bathroom as she stumbled and sank to the floor, she yelled for Harold as loud as she could. The next thing she felt was his hot, hard hand against her face. She mumbled to him that she had taken too many sleeping pills and she really didn't want to die. He then called her Aunt Freda, whom Pam had been raised by from two years old, to tell her to come quickly. Pam had evidently overdosed on pills.

Freda hurried to Harold's and Pam's home to find her sitting in the basement in a pair of wrinkled pajamas. She commanded Pam to get into her Cavalier, in the driveway; she was going to the hospital. On the way there Pam sank into a deep sleep from which she couldn't be awakened, Freda stopped and picked up a friend who would try to awaken Pam while she made the thirty to forty minute drive to the Berea Hospital. As Freda pulled into the parking lot at the hospital she wondered how many pills Pam had taken and how long ago she had taken them. Freda fled into the hospital to return with a nurse and a doctor. The doctor told Freda he could find no pulse but tried time after time to revive her. Pam faintly raised her hand which immediately indicated to him that she was going to be fine. With that she was rushed to the hospital only to be watched and probed for the rest of the night. Eventually the doctor came out to tell Freda that Pam was stable and going to be alright. By this time Harold had arrived at the hospital. He told Freda to go on home and get some rest and that Jenny had come to sit with Wade while he was at the hospital.

The next morning Pam felt dark hands tug at her gown. She immediately jerked her gown back down with her eyes closed. She couldn't manage to open them she was so tired. The hands won the fight and checked her heart and abdomen. She could feel the doctor's stethoscope on her body but couldn't see him. Pam soon drifted off back to sleep only to awaken an hour or two later to see Jenny standing at the foot of her bed. Jenny said, "Hello Sleeping Beauty." Pam asked how she was. Jenny replied she'd sat up with Pam's little Wade half the night and was pretty tired. Pam mumbled words back to her but faintly could get them out as her family doctor walked through the door. Dr. Isaacs was medium built but good looking with dark straight hair and a beard. Jenny wanted to know if this was the famous Dr. Isaacs she'd heard so much about. Pam didn't respond to her sister's remark but held out her hand for Dr. Isaacs to come and stand beside her. The only words she could understand him to say was Bluegrass Ridge in Lexington, Kentucky. Pam was going some place in Lexington because she had taken too many pills. This was the last thing she wanted. She really wanted to go home to her family. Jenny was leaving soon and said Harold would be over sometime in the evening to pick her up. She kissed Pam softly and told her she loved her, and that she would be over to Lexington to see her.

Chapter 3

As Pam was dressing, her tall bronzed husband came in to see her. She immediately ran over to hug him, but he stopped her and wanted to know if she was ready to go to Bluegrass Ridge. She felt a chill go up and down her spine that she'd never felt before. He was cold and abrupt with her. She immediately stopped in her tracks while trying to tell him at the same time she wanted to go home. He wouldn't listen. He said the doctor had recommended for her to go. Harold said, "I'll see to it that you'll go." The car ride to Lexington wasn't a pleasant one. Pam was uneasy the whole way. Harold was unusually quiet. Words very rarely passed between them. The air in the red Chevrolet Blazer was stale and lifeless. They both smoked and it was too much for one human body to take for very long. They had his and her Blazers. His was black and mysterious; hers was red and flamboyant. They always drove hers on long trips because it was more dependable than the black older model. Pam finally broke the ice by asking if Wade was ok. Harold replied, "He's fine but wanted to know if he could come along with her to the hospital. Pam said, "I don't see anything wrong with him riding along. Its good for him to see that people have problems that need worked out by someone other than family members." Harold didn't see things this way because he was silent the rest of the way. Traffic bothered Pam extremely bad. The big trucks that passed them had sayings on them that seemed to apply to her such as overnight, Pegasus, and the color yellow for scared. She knew they didn't know she was alive, but deep down she wanted them to know. She wanted them to know Wade was her son too. So many times she felt left out and ignored. Harold got to play with Wade while she cooked dinner or did laundry. Wade always did "man things" with Harold. He hardly ever brought Wade to her and said, "What is mommy cooking up tonight?" or "What pair of pants is mommy washing? Make sure they are clean from the laundry." She was never referred to as mommy but always referred to as Pam. Her thoughts were running rapidly as they pulled into the parking lot of Bluegrass Ridge. Pam hadn't even noticed how they got there or what street they had turned to find the place. It was somewhat remote. It was surrounded by trees and grass. There were other buildings close by it. Their parking lots weren't full or busy with cars going around in circles to find a parking space. Harold didn't drop her at the front door but went with her to the front lobby. Later he pushed open the door that led to a room at Bluegrass Ridge that seemed sound-proof to Pam. A woman came in and introduced herself while Pam lay lifeless on the couch.

Harold wondered if Pam had even understood or heard her name. He raked through Pam's purse desperately to find her insurance card. This hospital was an expensive one that would cost plenty of money. Harold hoped the insurance would pay for all it. It would probably take most of their savings if it didn't. He handed the insurance card to the woman nervously and asked how long she thought Pam would have to stay there. The woman answered, "She'll be here until the doctor feels it safe for her to return home and be with her family. She should be stable in a couple of weeks. Harold knew that only the doctor would determine her stay there. After the woman left, Harold reached for Pam's hand as she lay with soggy teardrops upon her face. She seemed not to realize the consequences of what she'd done the night before. He was angry with her and wondered why she turned small issues into large ones. Why did things have to matter to her so much? She only begged to return home and everything would be alright. She constantly wanted t o know if he and Wade still loved her. She loved them, why didn't they love her?

Pam thought the room was cold, so she reached for the warmth of Harold's arms. He only pushed her away angrily shifting from one side of the couch to the chair. Pam could see his mouth moving but couldn't understand the words coming from his lips. As she scooted closer, a woman came into the room, which startled her. Pam curled into a ball on the right side of the couch as her husband talked with the nurse. The nurse finally left the room. Harold stood up and led her through the door to more doors that opened into a hallway with a counter. The counter led to more doors which reached to a huge dayroom with a television. The television was on, but Pam very rarely could make out the words that came rushing at her. She turned to run to Harold, but he wasn't there to comfort her. People's voices were around her as she was being lead down a hallway. At the end of the hallway to the right was a room with two beds that she was supposed to stay in. The room had no television but a bathroom of its own.

The next morning Pam was led to a cafeteria filled with different kinds of breakfast foods. She chose Rice Krispies to eat. She barely tasted the cereal as it washed down her throat with a carton of juice. The orange juice was cool and sweet. It was good as she hadn't had anything to eat or drink the day before. The people sitting next to her chatted continually about things they had experienced. Some of them asked her what her name was. She mumbled, "Pam Combs." Someone asked, "Have you seen a doctor yet?" She breathlessly replied that she hadn't. Pam slowly got up and tried to make her way back to the room where she'd slept the night before. An Afro-American led her back to her room. The room was far away from the cafeteria so she had to think to get from one place to the next. "Let's see you walk up the hallway through the dayroom and counter room. Down the hall to…" "Mrs. Combs Dr. Stover is here to see you. Come this way and I'll show you his office." When Pam entered the office, there was no one there. She chose to sit on the couch that was the farthest away from the desk. The desk was small and against the wall. Dr. Stover introduced himself as he entered the room. He asked if she was Mrs. Combs. She answered him with a "Yes." This was the beginning of a long series of questions that Pam answered the best she could. She couldn't ask any questions back because he distracted her train of thought with pens, and drawers opening and closing. This kept her attentive as he asked questions that she knew she didn't know the answers to. Dr. Stover ended the session while opening the door. To her surprise he led her to her room, yet reassured her that he would be talking with her each day for awhile.

Pam mechanically walked to lunch and dinner only to return to her room. That evening she took a medicine called Wellabutrin. She took the medicine and swallowed its slick contents. This went on for days until she finally began to venture out of her room. Groups came first then socializing with her peers came. Slowly she began to respond to Dr. Stover with questions and answers. She began to tell stories about Wade, her family and her classroom. Pam wrote ideas in a journal that she preciously held in her hands at all times. She remembered her sister bringing clothes while visiting for an hour or so. The big event was when Harold brought Wade to visit. The visit was private and long. Wade wanted to talk to her alone, so they left the room to walk farther down the carpeted hallway. He crouched next to the wall a little shy; tears welled up in his eyes while he explained to her that he wanted her to come home. Pam's lips brushed his cheek as she replied, "I'll be home soon sweet peas." His little fleshy arms seemed to surround her as he hugged her around the neck. She smiled and pulled him closer to her. "Wade, it's always been you and me. It will always be you and me. I love you more than anything." While tears wet the top of her son's cap Pam said "Goodbye."

Harold and Wade picked up Pam three weeks later to find her cheerful and talkative. The drive home was pleasant. The Blazers warm heater fought the cold winter air as they drove along watching the snow cling to branches of trees in Jackson County. It was beautiful in the winter as snow and ice decorated the hills with their natural array of purity. The roads curves seemed to climb but yet quickly descend as they drove. A roller coaster ride couldn't be more thrilling than the ride that so contently brought them closer to the little town named Sand Gap. Pam and Harold both had been raised in Sand Gap. Wade loved his home and friends. People seemed to accept them back into their arms as they passed the sign that read the name of their hometown. Many people accepted them with open arms at the country gas station. Everyone spoke while they acknowledged that Harold, Pam, and Wade were back from the hospital. There wasn't a sign of indifference, or fearfulness as they entered into their precious homestead.

Pam's in-laws awaited her arrival. Foods and gifts covered the counter top of their snack bar. She slowly tugged at her coat then directed herself toward the living room in the back of the house. Their house plan was designed to comfort them as they saw fit. The kitchen overlooked a hillside covered with trees. The room had double doors that led out to an extravagant deck where they lounged in the evenings. The house was only about fourteen to fifteen hundred square feet but spacious enough for three people to live comfortably. The only thing they wished they had done differently was to have built a full basement instead of half basement to hold a pull in garage. The house was decorated to meet a country living type theme yet a few modern elements were thrown in to give character to the home. Harold's basement contained many CD'S, records, television, stereo system and Rolling Stone magazines. Her son's room was made up of bunk beds, desk, television, and toys that included X-men to Power Rangers. Pam's room consisted of a four poster queen sized cherry bedroom set. It was soothing for each of them to have their favorite space to blunder around in.

Little did Pam realize she almost lost everything that ever mattered to her in a matter of minutes? The wreck and the pills seemed unimportant as she thought how dear her home was to her. Could she stay well enough to make Harold and Wade happy again? This was a question that only the future could answer.

Chapter 4

Days were filled with KERA, laundry and pleasing Wade. The spring entered with an array of bright blossoms and a variety of brilliant green vegetation. The chilly winds reminded Pam of the cold winter's final blast of cold air. Day to day life was normal yet serene as the family enjoyed the countless hours of work and play. The foggy memory of last winter had passed. People in the community were making ready their gardens for the summer treats it would bring. School days seemed shorter as they approached summer. Summer meant a three month vacation that would begin when school ended. Wade would be a year older in the summer. His birthday was June 23, 1990. He would be eight or nine years old. Pam felt a bitter sadness come over her. She'd almost ruined his birthday. How could she be sick when she had so much to live for?

Her relationship with Harold and Wade both fell back into place. Time was on her side. She only had life to enjoy. Teaching came easy for her as it once had. The summer always gave her time to prepare for the following year. She was captivated in her son's basketball practices, baseball tryouts and swimming lessons. Berea was the perfect place for him to excel at these sports. The Camel Center had a nice basketball court and huge indoor Olympic sized pool. A yearly pass would allow them to enjoy swimming throughout the seasons. Twice to three times a week would be enough to fill their week with relaxation, as well as, exercise. Pam always took pride in involving Wade with sports that he was good at and interested in. Harold played golf with him twice weekly. He had done this with Wade since he was five years old. Pam occasionally rode the golf cart to delight in his progress. Summer had flown by. The festivities filled the days as they approached fall. School would soon begin an adventure with new students and new material.

The days were longer as Thanksgiving approached. Pam's nights started with restlessness then sleep in the later hours. Rest seemed to be an essential part of her life that she wasn't getting. She tried to wear herself down with teaching, caring for her family, and visits to the swimming pool. The corner in the basement seemed to fill with cobwebs as it awaited her return. She didn't want to go there during her sleepless nights, so she made the couch upstairs her last retreat. The covers seemed to bind her twisted body every night as thoughts of school, swimming and grocery shopping spun through her head. The grocery shopping seemed to attract people that stared at her every move. She would trample through the aisles only to find more faces looking at her. Pam wondered if the attire she wore was distasteful. Then she thought maybe she was studying their facial expressions so much that she'd been staring at them. Wal-Mart had always been her favorite place to shop. It had everything she loved to shop for. Pam wasn't an extravagant spender but liked buying things that were a reasonable price. Wal-Mart seemed more like a person to her rather than a concreted building. Harold and Wade enjoyed looking at toys and fumbling around with their sports equipment. Pam spent hours in Wal-Mart. It wasn't a thing of going there to get what she needed and get out. She studied prices and ingredients of foods. This was a pastime for her. The crowds of people became so intent that she began to shy away from spending so much time there.

As it grew nearer to Thanksgiving, the nights became a curse. Harold seemed to reach for her less and less during the night. They usually made love just after nine o'clock. Wade would go to sleep on the couch in the basement while Harold and she made love in her bedroom. As the nights seemed to grow longer she enjoyed making love around four in the morning. Her endless nights of not sleeping ended up with no love making as she was lying on the couch alone in the living room. Her thoughts bound her there. They wouldn't unleash her to go back to her bedroom. Her thoughts were usually disrupted by the slamming of cabinet doors. The doors slammed as Harold often prepared his own breakfast. He didn't like to eat her breakfast so he prepared his own the way he wanted. He left Pam and Wade to fend for themselves. This seemed harsh to Pam as she loved to prepare his breakfast. She only tried to brush it off as a phase he was going through. She often wondered why he didn't prepare theirs too. Tears trickled down her face because she knew he had grown tired of her. He just didn't love her anymore. Pam was a good cook. Harold didn't want her to use much sugar, oil or salt. He wanted to watch his weight, so she tried to abide to his picky habits. He wasn't overweight and wanted to stay that way. She had put on a few pounds while taking the Wellabutrin but it wasn't a significant amount. Pam had always been slender built. She very rarely watched her intake of calories. She usually walked them off. Swimming had toned her muscles to where her stomach was reasonably flat. Harold's build was the same since he got a lot of exercise playing golf three or four time a week. As they grew farther apart, their conversations consisted of remarks that lashed out at the other.

Harold informed Pam that she needed to go back to the hospital. She spent most of her nights awake in the living room while he tried to sleep. Her restlessness in the bed often woke him to the point where he couldn't go back to sleep. He encouraged her to get up and try to sleep in the living room. She seemed hurt that he'd grown tired of her scrambled eggs and toast that she prepared for breakfast. Pam didn't seem to understand that she was getting older. Oatmeal was better for his health and weight. He was growing tired of the long periods without conversation. Pam seemed preoccupied with something. He wondered if she was interested in someone else or if it was her sickness. They had gotten along well until the leaves began to color the hills in Jackson County. The fall seemed to bring about changes in her that resembled the changes that overwhelmed her the past winter. Maybe her medicine wasn't working anymore. She seemed involved with Wade but strayed off into a world he couldn't comprehend. He couldn't help her join his world because he couldn't really tell what she was thinking about to bring her back to reality. She stared for long intervals at people and objects that surrounded her. She caught only fragments of a sentence and responded with answers that made no sense. The answers usually pertained to her or Wade. They didn't include him. Was her mind so cluttered with other interest that he was left out? He didn't want to become alien to her, so he suggested she go back to the hospital. Pam seemed agreeable to what he wanted. He called Dr. Stover and explained to him that Pam's condition had become worse. Dr. Stover told Harold to bring her to Bluegrass Ridge and he could evaluate her there. Pam packed a few clothes but not enough for any length of time. So Harold threw in a few more things. They had washers and dryers at Bluegrass Ridge, but he didn't know if she would be able to use them for awhile.

Chapter 5

Dr. Stover met Pam in the lobby. She walked in alone this time. Dr. Stover seemed glad to see her as she smiled at him. Harold had jumped the gun this time. Her sleepless nights could have been taken care of in Dr. Stover's office rather than the hospital. She knew deep down this would be a short visit. When she studied Dr. Stover's face she got the impression he might agree with her. She wanted to prove to Harold this time that she could get well and stay well. Dr. Stover mumbled something nice to her as he led her to her room. Her room was closer to the dayroom than last time. She turned and walked into the dayroom which was very familiar to her. Nothing had changed; the room was covered with couches and large cushions. Bluegrass Ridge didn't seem as crowded this time. It was nearing Thanksgiving, people wanted to visit with their families. Pam knew she would miss Thanksgiving with her family. Why couldn't this have been an office call rather than a hospital visit? She didn't understand why she had fallen into a pattern of sleepless nights with racing thoughts. This time she knew what it was. She didn't have to go to groups to recognize her symptoms. All Harold had to do was helping her and make a doctor's visit. This time he dropped her off to see to herself. She wasn't sure what Dr. Stover would do this time. She figured he would keep her a couple of weeks to get her back on track. The three month visits to his office were very beneficial. Maybe this time things would be set in the right direction for good. She sure wasn't going to get all settled in to stay for awhile. She knew she had to listen more to recover by Christmas. She didn't want to let Christmas get by her.

Pam's sister Jenny had given her a phone card months ago that she hadn't used. She used the card to call Jenny. Jenny didn't know Pam was back in the hospital. She told Pam she would come and visit the next day. Pam hung up the phone only to pick it up again. This time she called Wade and talked with him. He told her that he would be over to visit as soon as Daddy would bring him. Pam asked, "Sweet Peas, can I speak to Daddy for a minute?" Harold's deep voice sounded harsh to her as she listened to him say "Hello." She asked Harold if anything was wrong, He replied, "I'm sorry Pam but I can't help you." Pam replied, "What do you mean I can't help you?" He told her that he wanted a divorce when she returned home from the hospital. Pam began to cry out over the phone "Please, please don't leave me; give me another chance. I'll do better the next time." He said he would bring Wade over to see her, that he still wanted a divorce when she was well enough to file for both of them. She was dumbfounded when he hung up on her. She sat in the floor holding the phone and wept until her whole body seemed dampened by her tears. A large Afro American came over to her and lifted her from the carpeted floor. He said, "Mrs. Combs." softly as he carried her to a room that had no windows. He and a lady sat with her for awhile. She continued to weep over and over and say, "Please, please, please....don't leave." Another woman came into the room and told her to lie down on the pad. She placed a pillow under Pam's head and left her crying. The door closed, the room wasn't dark and seemed stuffy. Pam couldn't tell how long she lay in a puddle of tears, but it seemed only minutes until she stopped to fall asleep.

"Dr. Stover is here to see you." The nurse told Pam early that morning. She led her to a room that had a big swivel chair. The desk sat in front of the chair. It couldn't hide the chairs many buttons. There was a picture of a horse hanging above the chair, someone at Bluegrass Ridge liked horses. Dr. Stover quietly entered the room. He didn't speak until he became comfortably situated in the leather chair. Dr. Stover said, "How are you today?" Pam didn't elaborate on what had happened the evening before but began to have thoughts of suicide in her head. He asked again, "How are you Mrs. Combs?"

In a lowered voice she told him she was fine. He asked her many questions. Some she answered the best she could, others she gave no answers. She was overwhelmed with thoughts about herself. Soon the session ended. While he opened the door, Dr. Stover told her he would be talking to her for a couple of weeks. This meant she wouldn't be at Bluegrass Ridge much longer. Two weeks meant only fourteen days. She would be home in time for Christmas. She had no intention of moving out of her home before Christmas. She would show Harold how well she was.

Later that day Pam was given a new medicine call Seroquel. She didn't ask what type of mental illness it was for. Gladly, she took the pill with a small cup of water. She picked up the telephone and dialed Wade's telephone number. It didn't occur to her that Wade was at school. Pam knew it was hard for him to go to school and face his classmates. Pam never heard him complain one time about his friends asking him questions about his mother. He seemed to just take it as an every day event that his mother had to go to the hospital. She'd had two surgeries and mental illness since he'd been born. It was a way of life for him. The Seroquel made her sleepy for the first couple days. After a few days she was able to attend groups wash her clothes, take showers and socialize with other patients. Around the fourteenth of December a nurse called Harold and told him that Pam was ready to come home. Harold came and picked her up the following day. Wade came with him that evening as they arrived at Bluegrass Ridge.

The basement was silent as the television was off. Its block walls shut out the sound of traffic as Pam and Harold sat looking at each other. Wade was at Jenny's. Pam didn't fall to pieces this time when Harold asked her for a divorce. She held back the tears as she asked him if they could wait until after Christmas. His plan was for her to move out and take their furniture, life savings and the red Blazer. Pam didn't think things through while the words poured from his mouth. She only knew she agreed to do what was asked as long as she could stay for Christmas. It wasn't Harold that would be leaving but Pam.

The next day Pam called Aunt Freda and asked her if she knew a good divorce lawyer. Aunt Freda went on about how she knew Harold would file for a divorce. She deplored the idea that Pam was finding a lawyer, giving Harold the house, and property. Pam didn't argue with her but told her that she would buy a home when she moved out if he wasn't happy. There wasn't anything she could do to change that. The Seroquel made her brave. Her thought patterns were fuzzy. She was agreeable to his terms because she wanted peace.

Miss Smith introduced herself to Harold and Pam as she swung around in her small gray chair. Her office was located in McKee, Kentucky. It was at the small county seat in Jackson County. They both went over the terms of the divorce. Pam was to receive custody of Wade, fifty thousand dollars, half of the furniture and the red Blazer. Harold was to pay two hundred a month in custody, keep the house with its property, half the furniture and the black Blazer. She concluded that he had come out with more than she. She felt as if clouds were over her head. She and Wade were drifting along slowly as if they were floating on a raft in the sea. It was damp there not surrounded with water but little droplets of moisture that made their bodies cool rather than hot. Her train of thought was broken as she was asked to write a check for five hundred dollars to pay for Miss Smith's services. Miss Smith didn't show any contempt for Harold; she only commented that illnesses sometimes tear couples apart. It was sad that they couldn't work out their differences after eighteen years of marriage.

Chapter 6

Pam's brother-in-law, Phillip helped her move into the house. It was a house that she loved immediately when she walked through to investigate its every crevice. It was newly built by one of the local people at Sand Gap. It sat in a wooded subdivision just recently planned out by its owner. The owners sold the houses as they were being built or were placed in their lots. Pam's house was more isolated on a hill at the end of the subdivision. It had sandy colored brick decorated with a country green doors and shutters on the exterior. The house's interior was spacious with three large bedrooms, two baths, kitchen, dining area and a large living room with a vaulted ceiling. The dining area led off to a double garage. Pam paid eighty six thousand dollars for her and Wade's home. She went in debt forty-thousand dollars. Later she wished she'd bought an older, less expensive place. Eighty-six thousand dollars was expensive for living quarters in Sand Gap. She hoped on her teaching salary that her three-hundred and seventy-five dollar a month house payment wouldn't be too much. Her decisions weren't sensible. She didn't ask for advice; she just made decisions on her own without really thinking things through.

Life for the first month was pleasant. She and Wade filled their days with school, swimming and shopping. They walked to neighbors homes in the evening and slept during the night with uninterrupted sleep. Pam felt as though she were on top of the world; things were going good. She had met no one that appealed to her. Dating was the last thing on her mind. She still felt a stir of passion when Harold picked up Wade. She longed for Harold to ask if she would like to come along with them each time they drove off. Pam wondered if Harold was dating and who it might be. She felt just a tinge of jealousy. Three or four months passed and her wish came true. He finally asked if she wanted to go with them. She quickly said, "Yes." She loaded herself into his vehicle thinking this is my chance to show him things might work out. She was feeling courageous and gleeful. Dr. Stover had changed her Seroquel to Topamax a week or so before. She had begun to have sleeping problems on the Seroquel. This was a sign to Dr. Stover and her that it wasn't working properly. Her body seemed to reject medicines easily. The Topamax was helping her sleep better and feel calm.

Harold drove out to his home on Upper Drive Fork Ridge Road. Pam and Wade chatted about their day and how they were glad that Pam could come along. Pam's medicine seemed to be agreeing with her. She'd lost a lot of weight and seemed energetic. He often thought how he missed her touch. She always made love with him with a closeness that he couldn't describe. He had been her only lover. Deep down Harold didn't want her to find someone else. They'd been raised together as neighbors. She was kind to his grandpa Joe. Harold often heard the story of how she pulled the weeds around the chain link fence for a dime. Pam was a tall brunette, with big blue eyes. Her hair was short and always bounced as she walked. She wore cut off blue jeans for shorts. This showed her skinny tan legs. She often went barefoot every place she visited. He often wondered, as a boy, if she even owned a pair of shoes.

The chattering was stopped as the threesome entered their old home. Harold looked at Pam's face. He knew she was observing the messy room. She was always so neat and clean around the house. They talked and drank soda as the television told the evening news. Soon Pam seemed to become bored and asked if she could clean the windows upstairs. Harold told her he would love it. Wade changed the channel on the television after she left and became engrossed in one of "his shows" as they called it. Harold carefully made his way up the basement steps. He knew if he made love to Pam that this would indicate to her that he wanted to get back together. He wanted to be back with her at this point.

Pam and Harold made love on the bathroom floor. It wasn't exactly your most romantic spot but at least it was an attempt to show one another that they missed and loved each other. From this time on Pam was in bliss. Harold came to see her and courted her like he'd never done before. Their lovemaking was true love. They would sneak and find spots where Wade couldn't see or hear them. Wade knew though because he would act out little things to let them know he knew. He had been listening to them very quietly so they wouldn't know he was close by. Wade loved his parents and made fun of them every chance he got. Wade had the feeling that Daddy would be moving in with them before too long. He was constantly asking questions about why they lived apart. Wade's happiness had always been a concern for Harold and Pam. She'd always attempted to please him even if it meant giving up her own interest somewhat. The spring was ending on a good note. Pam's yard was an interesting place to cook out on warm days. It was continuously filled with blossoming redbuds and dogwoods. The house had trees and all wooded areas around it. A neighbor called James mowed her yard at the beginning of the spring. Harold had his yard to mow. It was too much to ask him to mow both places. Pam could mow herself, but the yard was much too rough for her to push and pull at a lawn mower. Harold had done some landscaping for her but needed to do more. Hopefully he would be around this summer to complete his project.

Pam sat on the back deck crying. She'd been pregnant before but never this old when she tried with Wade. Dr. Stover talked with her and tried to soothe her by saying he knew a really competent doctor who would see to her if she were pregnant. Pam didn't tell him she'd been having sleepless nights this time because she just knew she might be pregnant. The long nights seemed unimportant compared to this. She'd had surgery a couple of years after Wade was born which left her unable to have children. They told her the surgery promised a ninety-eight percent chance that she couldn't conceive another child. At one time it was upsetting to her not to be able to have children again. They had lost a child before she had gotten pregnant with Wade. She'd gone to the doctor's office on a regular visit. She lacked a week being eight months pregnant. The baby hadn't moved any before the appointment. The doctor asked how she was and she told him she was fine but she was a little worried something was wrong. She hadn't felt Jobie Benjamin move for a whole day. The doctor explained that as she got bigger that the baby would move less and less. Harold had come with her on this visit because he was uneasy too. No words can explain how they felt or reacted when the doctor told them the baby had passed away. She had the baby in a Lexington hospital. He was buried in Combs graveyard at Chestnut Flat. They both visit the grave every Memorial Day. Pam didn't know how far along she was, but she just knew she was pregnant again. Then she had Wade. Her train of thought was broken when the doorbell rang several times. She finally answered it. It was Harold. They were alone. Wade was gone to Jenny's. Pam led Harold out back to the deck. There she told him she thought she was pregnant. His reaction was totally opposite to hers. He seemed glad. He told her that he would like to move back in. He didn't see it as a way to capture him again. Pam still didn't want to be pregnant. The medicine she was taking might cause the baby not to be normal she told him. She just wasn't able to have another child. Harold said he would help more with this one. Wade was old enough to help with a baby too. Pam didn't tell Harold, but to her Wade was still a baby himself. Harold stayed longer that evening. He was attentive and understanding. She couldn't believe her ears as he talked about wanting another baby and wanting to move in with her and Wade. She thought at one time their relationship was completely over. It all was jumbled together in her mind. She thought while Harold talked. She seemed not to hear sentences only a word every now and then. She didn't explain to him how she was feeling. This time it was different; the thoughts seemed like words rather than thoughts. It was like something or someone was telling her to say she might be pregnant. Was she lying to herself and to others to get what she wanted? She had never actually lied to anyone before. All she knew was the racing thoughts made her very fatigued. Harold left with a good-night kiss. His lips brushed hers as he got into his Blazer. The starry sky seemed to reach out to her as it was time for her to go inside to her bedroom.

Pam awoke from her sleep around two in the morning. Then she found her way to the living room couch. She meant not to smoke as she stared at a pack of cigarettes. She didn't smoke when she was pregnant with their other two children. She didn't pick the cigarette pack up. She ignored it as she lay on the couch trying to go back to sleep. Harold was going golfing the next morning. He said he should be leaving early that he probably wouldn't call before he left. It was the beginning of June the days were hotter than the evenings, so she told him to take plenty Gatorade with him. She lay in the darkness thinking first of Harold then of Wade. Jenny said she going to come by early with Wade because she had a horse to drop off at a friend's house. Jenny loved horses. She had a small horse farm that she treasured. The horses with her job kept her active and busy. Jenny hadn't let Pam ride any of their new horses; they were high spirited and full of life. She told Pam she was afraid she'd fall off of them because her balance wasn't as good as it used to be. Pam thought at the time she was being frivolous. Now she knew that Jenny was just trying to protect her. As children Jenny always seemed to intervene when Pam began to make poor judgments. She would never let her climb to high up a tree or condone it when she found out that Pam was trying to smoke but always was trying to get her not to smoke. She never told on her but always found a way to make Pam stop doing things that might be self destructive. She was a very special big sister. Harold seemed to take over her role when they first married. He was always giving advice on things. Pam loved them both desperately. When she was alone with her thoughts, nothing she thought of seemed to ease her mind. She wished they there all the time.

The doorbell rang many times before Pam awakened enough to answer it. She peeked through the crack only to find Wade and Jenny standing there with Wade's bag of clothes. Jenny told her that Wade might want to go back to sleep that he and Jason had stayed up most of the night.

Pam was very sleepy and thanked Jenny for having him in their home. She told Jenny that she was really all the family she had besides Harold's brother and sister. They were getting older and if anything happened to Harold and Pam that Jenny would have to look after Wade. Jenny smiled and told her she would see them in the next couple of weeks. Little did Jenny know Pam was having another episode with her bipolar condition, Pam was trying to hide it. Wade entered the house and seemed whiny. She tried to get him to eat eggs for breakfast but he only pushed the plate away. Then she tried cereal. Pam told him he was acting like a baby. She ended up spanking his leg with her hand. That didn't work so she tried to lay down with him. That didn't work so she explained to him that he was a big nine year old boy now and it was time that he acted grown up. Nothing seemed to satisfy him. She finally gave up and lay back down on the couch. As he pulled and tugged at her all morning she became more agitated. She finally yelled at him to leave her alone, that she was sick. Pam trotted to the back room to use the telephone. She called Hanna at the crisis line to ask if they could send an ambulance to take her to the hospital. Hanna said she would try to get the ambulance there within the next couple of hours. She asked Pam a few questions and decided she needed to go back to Bluegrass Ridge. She wanted to call ahead of them to make arrangements. Pam told her she was there alone with Wade. Hanna must have called Freda because Freda arrived only minutes after the phone call. Freda had a large basket with lunch foods in it. She had worked most of the morning on homemade soup. Pam didn't eat anything, but Wade filled his belly full of soup and crackers. He went to lie down, but Freda told him that he was coming home with her until Harold could return from his golfing trip that Pam was going to the hospital. Pam reassured him that it wasn't his fault that she'd been having a hard time before he came home. As she entered the ambulance she kissed Wade and told him how much she loved him. He was pitiful standing there with Freda as she drove off.

On the way to Lexington, she thought of suicide. To keep the thought from dancing around in her head she would tell herself to fight for her sanity while the voices laughed at her and told her to give up everything that she held so dearly. She wished she could be a better mother for Wade. She was in a constant fight between fatigue and psychosis. She imagined she was pregnant. How would she know? Pam stumbled out of the ambulance as the driver lead her into Bluegrass Ridge. She didn't know the way there anymore. There wasn't anyone there to greet her. She made the decision to go into the hospital. Maybe the insurance would pay for it, maybe it wouldn't. At this point she really didn't care what anyone thought. All she knew was that she needed help to sleep and sort things out. The voices in her head had made themselves clear. She stuck her fingers in her ears to block their sounds. She couldn't fight thousands of voices that rushed at her from every direction. They were telling her bad things that she didn't want to hear.

Pam spent three to four weeks on the isolation ward. Her every move was monitored. She was helped with her meals and bathing. The rest of the time she lay in a bed covered with white starched sheets. The Lithium slid down her throat twice a day. Blood levels were taken weekly. As soon as the Lithium began to take effect she was moved out into a room with other patients. The day room was very familiar to her as were the group rooms. She couldn't remember talking with Dr. Stover over the last couple of weeks, but she was sure she had spoken with him. Pam stayed at the Ridge eight weeks which was equivalent to two months. She'd spent practically her whole summer break in the hospital. Lithium was a mood stabilizer which worked well in bipolar patients. Dr. Stover had finally diagnosed her as being bipolar. This was an illness she'd probably have her whole life. It just worsened and needed treatment as she got older. Deep down Pam felt that she needed something more for anxiety. She became easily excited when she had racing thought telling her untruths.

Wade grabbed her around the neck and slung her across the room laughing. He was glad to see her. He always liked to roughhouse with her. He's done this since he was small. His daddy usually got the best of him, while she just let him sling her all over the place. Bluegrass Ridge always seemed glad to see Wade. They'd given them their privacy when they needed to talk. Talking wasn't as comforting as actions though. Pam wished she could show him how well she could be instead talking to him about her illness. Pam didn't want to have an illness. She had a hard time accepting the fact that she had inherited a mental illness. She went to college practically with no help and become a successful teacher with rewards. Wade was a handsome intelligent boy that she'd given birth to. Why couldn't things just be? Why did the world around her become cluttered with complications? It was time for her to go home.

Wade was outside playing baseball with one of the neighbor's son. Harold was sitting in the living room talking with her. She just knew he was going to say it was time for them to break things up again. To her surprise he didn't do this. He explained that he still wanted to get back together, "The end of August would be a good time for me to move in," he said. It was Labor Day weekend and he would have three days to move his things. He didn't want to have to take time off from his teaching. Pam didn't want to have to take off either. She'd used enough of her days in the hospital. She usually saw Dr. Stover at the end of the day. His secretary had been very cooperative about saving her evening visits. The visits didn't cut into Pam's sick leave days. She usually went to the doctor every three months unless she was having trouble with her sleep. This time she should sleep because Dr. Stover had given her Ambien along with the Lithium. Pam felt settled and comforted as she imagined how they would move Harold's belongings. She would gloat at the chance to help him move in. Placing his things around the house would give them both a satisfaction she'd been longing for. He seemed anxious to move.

Chapter 7

Harold, Pam and Wade filled their days with work, golfing, shopping, school, and visiting with family and friends. Their first Christmas in the new house was everything they'd hoped for. They'd picked out green Christmas lights to cover the tree and inside the windows. There was a wreath on the door sprinkled with little green lights to match the tree and windows. They visited with Pam's family and Harold's on Christmas Day. They went their separate ways to eat a large meal for lunch. They met at Harold's mother and dad's to open gifts and pass money back and forth to each other. Wade usually ended up with the most because he was the youngest member of Harold's family. Pam's family usually just ate their meal and visited. Her family wasn't as fortunate with money as Harold's. Pam and Harold loved picking out Christmas gifts for Maude and Burlon, They were older; it was fun to pick them things out to wear to church. Pam and Harold didn't usually attend church with them unless it was Mother's Day. Pam's family attended different churches so she never went with them on any special occasions. Freda, Pam's aunt went to the same church as Maude and Burlon sometimes. Her and Wade would go every now and then to please all three of them. Wade loved Christmas. He'd always got up at the crack of dawn to open presents and tear in to envelopes filled with money. Wade enjoyed being with each parent as they sneaked around to buy a gift for the other one. He always knew what both were getting for Christmas. The family didn't spend bunches of money on Christmas but tried to pick out the gifts that were special to the other. Christmas, the first year after they got back together was special because the whole family got to be together with the in-laws. Even though Pam and Harold hadn't remarried yet it felt like it used to feel after Wade was born. The first six or seven years of his life were exciting and rewarding for everyone. The last four or five years had been fun, but everyone worried, deep down, that Pam's mental illness would effect him in a way that they couldn't fix. He seemed well adjusted no matter which parent had caused him sadness. Pam had saddened him with her hospital visits, while Harold had saddened him by asking for a divorce. Wade still acted happy and loved both his parents. It showed it through his eyes, smile and school work. His stories he wrote at school were very creative. Most of them were about things he'd made up, yet some were about different individuals in his family: All were about someone or something he loved. They all looked forward to the following year. Things were going in the right direction.

Pam had been to Wal- Mart to buy groceries for that week. She got out of her car and grabbed a couple of bags of groceries. As she walked on the sidewalk to the front door she glanced down. There lay curled up was a rather large snake poking its head at her. The snake was dark with white splotches on the top of its neck and its head. Pam jumped while dropping the groceries to the ground. She ran and opened the door to the room that was underneath her house. She reached for a shovel only to return to find the snake gone. It looked poisonous to her. She was going to kill the snake with a shovel. Growing up as a girl there had always been snakes in their yard. They were taught that snakes could be dangerous and you must kill them with a hoe or a shovel. Many people believed that snakes were an important part of the food chain; you shouldn't kill them unless they are a threat. She wasn't going allow it to live near her front door and scare her to death. She looked wildly through her flowers to find the snake. It had evidently left when she rushed to get the hoe. Later, that evening, Pam told the snake story to Harold and Wade. She instructed Wade to try and kill it with a hoe if he saw it. She wanted him to come and tell her first though. She wasn't sure how he would go about killing it. They got the hoe out and Pam demonstrated to Wade, on how to strike at its neck. They used an old stick as a snake. She showed him how to stand behind it rather than in front of the snake. She explained that if he stood in front of the snake it might strike and bite him. When he heard this he told her that he would rather run and get her or daddy one to kill the snake. He sounded a little cowardly. A week or two after they had cautioned him about snakes, Pam was preparing dinner. She heard Wade outside yelling. She ran to the front porch only to find him pounding the ground with his golf club. She immediately screamed "Snake!" She ran to him in her bare feet to find a baby snake cut in half. The upper part of its body scooted through the grass. The lower part of its body twisted and flopped underneath Wade's golf club. She grabbed the club and began to search frantically for the upper part of the snake's body. When she found it she pounded the top of the snakes head vigorously. She knew it was dead, but she kept pushing and pounding with the club. Wade grabbed the club out of her hands and began to make chopping motions with it. After a few minutes, Pam told Wade she thought the snake was dead, that he could stop now. The snake was just a baby but had teeth. She knew babies had come from the snake she had previously tried to kill. She cautioned Wade about chopping a snake in half and how it might still be able to bite. With that they returned inside of the house. Boy, did they have s story to tell Harold at dinner that night.

Summer had crept up on them. It was time for Wade's baseball game. He had begun practice a couple of weeks before school let out. Now it was time for their second game. The game was at McKee's baseball field. It was a small field but served the community's needs. Pam was delighted that she didn't have to go to the hospital this summer. She had missed practically all of Wade's games last year. Wade played shortstop and first baseman. He was rather impressive as a catcher. He loved most sports, but had a hard time fitting them all in as the seasons often overlapped with one another. Pam sat on the bench yelling, "Go Wade go!" each time he caught or hit the ball. Harold was in the dugout with the other fathers helping the coach make plays and give out signals to his team. Wade's team was named the Bearcats. The boys had voted on what they wanted to be called as a team. "That wasn't a damn strike!" Nancy yelled. Nancy was Pam's friend. Pam had made friends with her at the ball games. What she liked about Nancy was she never questioned Pam about her mental illness. She seemed like a sensitive person with what time she wasn't cussing the umpire a blue streak. The umpire seemed to take glee in making Nancy mad. They yelled and screamed at every play. It looked as though Wade's team was going to win. Pam looked down the long row of benches to see Freda hurriedly approaching them. Pam knew something had to be wrong. Freda never attended any of Wade's sporting events. She scampered down the bench to meet her halfway. "Harold's mom, Maude, had a stroke!" Freda said breathless. Pam ran to the dugout to tell Harold to go to his mom's side that she'd been taken to a Lexington hospital. The ambulance driver told Burlon that he thought it was a stroke. Harold sped out to the parking lot quickly as Pam gathered up Wade. Freda drove them home. As she drove she told Wade stories about his grandma and grandpa. She talked about their visits with each other and things they said and done on their visits. It settled him down. He looked scared that Maude had suffered a stroke.

Wade could barely remember Freda's husband lying bed ridden from a heart attack. Freda told how Uncle Ralph used to reach out to touch Wade. He often acted as though he knew Wade but didn't know anyone else. They figured out that Wade was at eye level and this made Ralph able to see him more clearly. Uncle Ralph's funeral was the first funeral that Wade had ever attended. Wade was only a small boy during this time and told Aunt Freda he could barely remember Uncle Ralph, but he remembered being sad. Soon they pulled into the driveway to Pam's house. She thanked Freda as she got out off the car. As soon as she got home she went to her room to say a prayer for Maude. She asked Wade if he wanted to come with her. He told her he had rather say a prayer in his own room. She understood and said things would be ok that his granny was a strong woman.

Maude was on the critical list and in the Lexington hospital. She couldn't speak, dress or feed herself. After a couple of weeks she was moved to Berea hospital's nursing home. There she was taken care of just about twenty-four hours a day. She seemed not to know people but would reach for them as they came to stand close to her bedside. Wade and Harold were visiting one day while Wade was there he watched death pull the air slowly from Maude's lungs. She passed away before Wade's eyes. Pam was shocked that Harold let Wade witness this as Wade seemed awfully young to watch someone he loved pass away.

Wade seemed a little troubled but held up well as he was one of the pallbearers at the funeral. Wade sat on the front row of the left aisle while Harold sat on the first row of the right side. Pam sat in the back of the room with friends. She couldn't bear to make herself sit beside the family. For some reason she felt out of place. As the funeral began Pam thought of the quilt Maude had given her for Christmas. It had bright colors that matched the Christmas colors. Maude had told her not to say anything about the quilt to the family because she didn't want Harold's brother and sister to be hurt. Harold's brother and sister had always took interest in her and Wade. Why would they be hurt that she'd given her a special quilt? She thought of many things as the funeral progressed toward its end. She loved Maude and wished she was with them alive and breathing.

Pam barely remembered what was said during the graveside service. Pam was ashamed when she heard the dirt hit the casket. She knew she had become so engrossed in her own thoughts that she had missed the service. Her body was there but her mind wasn't.

Chapter 8

The rest of the year was a blur to the whole family. They seemed to go through the motions but weren't really there. It felt this way to Pam. Some of her nights were restless but not all. She started sleeping on the living room couch again. The medicine Dr. Stover had given her wasn't working for her. This time Pam was determined to work through her problems on her own. Each visit with Dr. Stover was short and to the point. She never brought up sleepless nights or racing thoughts to him. This went on for what seemed like eternity but was only a year and a few months. Dr. Stover and she discussed her applying for her teacher disability. He thought it was a good idea. She did finally apply in January. This wouldn't mean the end of her career but only a couple of years off. She received her disability in February. Pam meant to take off from work for only a little while. Pam had to apply for disability yearly until she was sixty. This was hard to do as she felt the closer to time to apply for it made her become more stressed out. She longed to go back and teach, but she gave up on the thought after Dr. Stover released her as a patient. She chose another doctor in Lexington that she liked equally as well. She had to stay under a doctors care to get her retirement papers filled out.

After a few years, Pam decided to go back to school. It was spring and she went to school to visit the principal to see if she would be allowed to come back to her old school. The school was under construction. As they tore down the old rooms they replaced them with new rooms.

It was interesting to see how they built the new school. Pam talked with some of the school personnel as she waited for the principal to arrive. It felt good to have conversations with people she knew from her school days. As she entered the teachers' lounge, two police officers approached her. She stuck out her hand to introduce herself to them. They didn't return the gesture. One asked Pam to follow them to an empty room in the building. While she was there, they began to search her person and her purse. She was so embarrassed she barely understood the things they were telling her. They told her that someone had called the central office and said she was making threatening remarks about having a gun and how she was going to shoot people with it. She asked them if this was a joke. She hadn't said anything about having a gun. They told her it was a felony to threaten people with a gun on school premises. She told them she hadn't done this. She was at school to see about getting her old job back. The police officers acted as though she were a common criminal. They searched the trash cans, desks and her car. They couldn't come up with a gun. They called Harold and he told them the only gun they owned was still hidden there at their house. "Mrs. Combs, we still have to take you in because this person said she heard you make a threat." Pam was told this by the officers. Pam told them that she had witnesses that would say she never made any threat towards anyone using a gun or anything else. They still took her to jail and set bond at five thousand dollars.

Pam had never even experimented with guns, drugs or alcohol. She never had so much as a parking ticket. That person that made the claim had lied about her. Evidently they didn't want her to be able to start teaching again. Pam spent a horrible night in jail. She spent time crying and saying, "Please let me go, I'm innocent."

They wouldn't even let her make a call home. What on earth did Wade and Harold think of her now. The deputies on duty that night sprayed mace in her face and threw her into the basement. They said she was bothering the other people with her crying. She had to rinse her face with water from the commode. She couldn't see to find the sink as she crawled along the cement floor. The next morning the bond on her was dropped. Aunt Freda came to visit. Pam sat in her lap crying. The sheriff told her that she was free to go. Freda wouldn't hush until they sent her to the psychiatric hospital in Hazard. Freda told Pam that she had to go to court. If she was evaluated by a doctor, it would be better for her when she showed up for court. A threat on school premises was considered a felony. Pam found it hard to believe that someone had told such a lie. She was driven to Hazard that morning. She stayed there for seventy-two hours for observation. The doctor there didn't change her medicine and showed up for court. He said he believed that she wouldn't be prosecuted because the police didn't find a gun. It sounded as if she was telling the truth. Hazard hospital was different than Bluegrass Ridge. It didn't have the big windows, carpeted floors or appealing lush couches. It had bedrooms with two beds and a bath. Its dayroom had hard plastic covered chairs. Pam had to sit almost the whole day. She was allowed to take a nap but not for very long. Pam didn't like it at Hazard's psychiatric ward. She wished she was at home. Harold would never forgive her. Even though it wasn't her fault it was embarrassing for Harold and Wade both. The hospital transported Pam home. No one in the family came to visit her. Harold and Wade returned home from school to find Pam sitting on the couch.

Harold sat down to talk to her while Wade hugged her around the neck. They were both convinced she'd said something at school to lead them to believe she was guilty. In tears she told Harold and Wade both she hadn't done anything to make threatening remarks.

They wouldn't believe her. She told them there was no sign of a gun; why wouldn't they believe her? The board didn't even remember who it was that had made the call. Why didn't they believe her? Harold said he was tired of her getting in trouble and having to go to the hospital. He and Wade had decided to leave the following weekend. She didn't want them to leave. She begged Wade to stay with her over and over. He only looked at his dad and said he would be going with him. Pam's heart was broken. All she knew was that she didn't want to live anymore.

Harold knew she would be lost without them. Why did he want to leave? Why couldn't he just believe her? He didn't want to believe her she decided. Was it the way she looked or dressed? She decided it was something else other than the incident. She actually thought there were two Wades. She didn't tell the doctor in Hazard this but had told Harold this. He acted as though she was making the story up. She couldn't stay well enough to hold things together, so she gave in to the racing thoughts and voices that she heard constantly. Harold and Wade moved out over the weekend. They took much of the furniture with them. She was left with half a living room set, a dining set and one bedroom suit. He took a couch and Television out of the living room, two bedroom suits and two televisions. Wade told her that he'd be back to visit.

During the next couple of weeks Pam went to court, sold her house, and longed to see Wade. The court set a grand jury hearing for the following month. Pam couldn't believe that the judge didn't drop the charges. Freda was there with her when the judge told her that she would have to meet with the grand jury. She was scared that they would convict her of a felony. This meant one to five years in the penitentiary. Pam felt as though she was a fairly meek and mild person. She had outbursts with her illness but they were never violent. She may be somewhat self destructive but would never harm another person. Her good name was destroyed. People looked at her funny when she went to the store, church or the gas station. She knew they were saying things like, "That's the one that made the threat at school." She tried to ignore the stares and go on about her life as though nothing had happened.

She sold her house for ninety-six thousand dollars and moved into an apartment in Annville. It was at the other end of the county. Pam thought the change might take her mind off the things that had led her to do this. She paid Wade's college tuition with some of the money. The other money she put on C.D.'s under his social security number and his name. He should have enough to send him to college if he didn't get awarded a scholarship. She had very little left to get by on. Her medicine and rent was expensive. She wished she was still teaching. Wade came to visit her about once or twice a week in the new apartment. She hoped kids weren't kidding him at school about his mother. It they were, he never let on. He was a strong boy for his age. He was now entering his teenage years. He was thirteen when he left to live with his dad. They rented a small house in Tyner. Tyner was six or seven miles away from where she lived. She would be able to run out and see Wade when she wanted. Harold agreed to let her do this. She paid no child support but paid his health insurance. Harold never went to court to get custody of Wade. He left the custody in her name for the time being.

Pam arrived for her grand jury hearing early that morning. She didn't want to be late. She wore a pair of tan pants, checked black and white vest, white blouse and black sandals. Gold and sliver belts hung from her waistline. She wore three of these narrow belts about everywhere she went. They had little rings that hung down on her hips. Two of the belts were gold while one was silver. Thoughts of what she had on danced through her head as she waited for the meeting. A tall thin officer stepped out of the room he said that the jury was waiting. He told her to come inside with him to the room. He led her to a seat next to the commonwealth of attorney. The attorney began to ask her questions as did the jury members. She answered the best she could. She knew they thought she was scared because the attorney was friendly and told not be frightened; they just wanted to hear her side of the story. She told them her side. She never once left the room for them to decide whether she was guilty or not. Evidently they had decided her innocence before she came into the room. The attorney smiled at her, and told her she was free to go. Her legs felt like paddles swishing through water as she walked out of the room. She was so happy that she drove directly to Harold's house first to tell him and Wade that she was free. They had gone to school when she pulled into an empty driveway. Later that evening she called Harold, Wade and her sister Jenny to tell them of the good news. They all acted delighted over the phone that she didn't have to go to prison. The people that the jury had questioned must have backed up her story that she was never alone with anyone long enough to have made a threat. She was free.

Pam's days were filled with cleaning her apartment, eating out, cooking for Wade once or twice a week, and walking to the little church about a mile away from her. Her walks got her interested in going to church there. So she began to attend regularly on Sunday mornings. The people there were polite and friendly towards her, and she felt at ease. This went on for about a year.

She'd had her teacher retirement papers filled out once since she'd lived in the apartment in Annville. The papers were a worry to her since she had to drive all the way to Lexington to see the doctor and nurse practitioner. She was so worried that she wouldn't get the retirement back. It never once crossed her mind to go back to school since the incident at school. It was hard for her to get by on her retirement check form month to month. She was happy in the apartment but couldn't afford the rent and bills that went along with the apartment. She began to look for another apartment that was cheaper. She found a low income apartment in McKee that was about a hundred and seventy-five dollars cheaper on the month. The drawback to the apartment was she would have to go to the laundry mat. She moved into the cheaper apartment anyway. She was able to save enough there to give Wade a little extra money. She didn't mind doing this because he as always thanked her as though he really appreciated the money. Harold had retired from teaching and didn't have as much money as he did when he taught school. They lived a high lifestyle because they golfed two or three times a week in London, Kentucky. Wade was good in golf and had joined a golf league at his school. At first Pam was happy in the new apartment complex. Her sister Rita lived directly behind her in a one bedroom apartment. They visited frequently and began to go places together.

Pam became interested in dating. No one had approached her for a date since she'd begun to live alone. Harold kept telling her to find someone as he had. She told him that no one had found her. The men she was attracted to were already married. She couldn't find anyone her age. One or two of her neighbors invited her to go to London, Kentucky dancing. The place they asked her to go to didn't serve alcohol, so she agreed. She met a man there who wasn't married and near her age. He wasn't what she thought of as handsome but he was nice to her so she agreed to go out with him. His name was Eddie. He came to see her on a Sunday. They were supposed to go to Natural Bridge. Eddie's car was old and broken down looking. That's all Pam needed was someone poorer than she was. When she saw the broken down car and his old pair of tennis shoes, she decided not to go to Natural Bridge. The car looked as if it might break down any minute. All seemed at a loss until she went to the gas station at McKee that week. A friend of hers that worked there told her that she knew a Mexican construction worker from Berea that would like a date with her. Pam agreed to meet him at a restaurant in Berea. She got there before he did and waited for his white truck to pull up. His truck wasn't new, but at least it looked as if it would run. When he got out of his truck she couldn't believe her eyes. He was neatly dressed. He was a little taller than her. He had wide shoulders with a slender body underneath. His big brown cow eyes took her breath away as he smiled and asked if she were Pam. She immediately threw out her hand and asked if he was Phillip. She asked, "Why do you have an American name?" He told her he was raised in California not Mexico. Pam was very pleased with her date. He wasn't a rich man but worked hard and spent his money wisely. They often talked on the telephone during the week and went to restaurants over the weekends. Pam really enjoyed his company. It was near Christmas when Phillip told her that he had to return to California to care for his parents. She wished so much that he wouldn't leave her. He promised to return to Kentucky and take her back with him. She said she would gladly go. He never returned as he said he would. He called Pam one night around ten o'clock to tell her that he had gotten back together with his old girlfriend. Pam was so disappointed that she felt like giving up on men. At least she still had Wade. She made sure that Wade loved his Christmas dinner at her apartment. He received presents, money and food. He was with her on Christmas Day even though everyone else was too busy or gone. She didn't let Phillip ruin her Christmas.

Later that winter Pam began going to an office in Jackson County to see a psychiatrist. He had hired one of the local men to be a therapist in his office. She knew the therapist and thought this would be a good time to switch doctors. She had received her retirement back in January. Pam didn't like driving all the way to Lexington. It was a long way and the gas was a big dent in her budget. Her first visit at the doctor was an interesting one. The therapist saw her first. He made her an appointment with the doctor. Her therapist, Mr. Harris, was pleasant. He explained that he was associated with Comprehensive Care in Jackson County. The office was actually located in the Comprehensive Care building. Pam told him the medicine she was taking and how she had been on that medicine for some time. She didn't tell him about her sleepless nights because she had other things that were more pressing. She explained to him how she was bored at home. He suggested that she come to Comprehensive Care three or four times a week to break the boredom of staying at home all the

Chapter 9

Pam's sleepless nights were occurring more frequently. She couldn't think straight because she had become so tired. She had taken Wade to his ball games but felt as though she wasn't really there. Fatigue had set in. She returned to see Mr. Harris a month later. It wasn't long until her appointment with the doctor would come around. Pam couldn't wait, so she called and asked to see the therapist. She told him of her sleepless nights and how she dwelled on the idea that there was more than one Wade. He didn't laugh or make fun of her but just listened. She told him that Wade wasn't Wade sometimes but a boy who looked similar. She explained how the boy wore almost identical clothes. She didn't have a name for him. What else could she do but call him Wade? She left the office a bit shook up. The therapist didn't say whether he believed her or not; he just listened attentively. He didn't tell her she was sick. She walked toward her car thinking he might have believed her. Pam called later that day to tell Harold she wasn't feeling well. She told him that she was still going to cook Wade his favorite meal for dinner. It was round steak with carrots, potatoes, celery and onions cooked around it slowly.

The vegetables simmered in the brown gravy from the steak as Pam awaited Wade's arrival. She had corn bread in the oven and strawberry pie in the refrigerator. Pam delighted in cooking for Wade. Harold had always told her she was a good cook. Wade ate so much that she thought his belly would pop. He lay down on the couch to snooze while his stomach was full of steak and pie. Pam lay down on the floor next to him and was able to nap for a few minutes. She always felt better when Wade visited. She felt he were someone else and had to act a certain way to keep him from knowing that she really thought he was another boy. She knew this sounded ridiculous. She couldn't help it. It had become second nature to her to cover up the fact that she thought someone had switched sons with her. Pam knew she had the real Wade next her. She'd made a complete fool of herself earlier that week calling lawyers offices to tell them that someone was switching sons with her. She said there was a boy who claimed to be Wade.

She blamed different people that she knew. She said they were trying to take away her custody from her. Freda had called her and tried to explain to her that there couldn't be two Wades. Someone had called Aunt Freda and told on her. Pam wouldn't listen and hung up the phone quickly. These thoughts were going over and over in her head as she waited for Wade to wake up. Harold soon came to pick up Wade. Wade kissed her when he left and told her that he loved the meal. She told him that she looked forward to cooking for him the next week.

The next morning Pam was taking a bath when she heard someone knocking at the front door. She climbed out of the tub and wrapped her snow white bath robe around her wet soggy body. She peeked out of the window to see two police officers standing at her front door. She opened the door to see what they wanted. They told her Comprehensive Care was worried about her because she missed an early appointment that day. She told them nothing was wrong; she just wasn't feeling well. They asked her to come along with them Mr. Harris wanted to talk to her. They drove her to Comprehensive Care where Mr. Harris asked her many questions. He told her that it would do her good to spend a couple of weeks in Hazard hospital. She really didn't want to go, but he told her that it had been court ordered and she must do what the court said for her to do. He felt that her medication needed adjusting, and he was afraid to do this outside of the hospital. She didn't fuss with him. She gave up and went along with the officer peacefully.

Pam spent two weeks in Hazard hospital. The doctor there felt that she needed to be on Risperdal. He told her that she was bipolar with psychotic features. Pam was released to go back to her apartment.

Their van brought her home to the apartment. They talked very little with her. She was just dropped off. She got into her car and drove to Rite-Aid to get her new prescription filled.

Pam was only home for a week when she called the state police. She reported that she had custody of Wade and that his dad wouldn't return him. The police went to the Courthouse; her custody papers clearly stated that she had custody of Wade. They went to visit with Harold. He told them it was true that he'd never filed for custody, but Wade chose to live with him instead of his mother. He said at the time she'd agreed to these terms.

They told him to file for temporary custody until he got full custody. They didn't return Wade to his mother. To their understanding she was mentally ill and had just gotten out of the hospital. Pam was angry that Wade didn't visit more. He never spent the night with her once after Harold left with him. The police tried to explain to her this was his choice. He was at the age that he could do what he wanted as long as there wasn't any abuse. They told her that Harold had gotten temporary custody until he could get full custody.

She got a letter in the mail telling her when to show up for court. She drove everywhere trying to find a lawyer. She went to McKee, Manchester, London and Richmond. All the offices that she visited said that Wade was twelve and could make up his own mind. There wouldn't be any use in her filing for custody. Pam showed up in court without a lawyer. She told the judge she'd tried to get a lawyer, but couldn't come up with one on such short notice. She told the judge that she only wanted to see Wade more. The judge gave Harold custody of Wade. He stated in the hearing that she didn't have to pay custody since she had given him money but was to pay his insurance until it ran out with the state department. He told Harold to make sure that she saw Wade more often. She agreed to these terms. Harold had full custody of Wade now. Pam returned to her desolate apartment. She wished that Harold loved her and would have taken her back. She could see that this wasn't going to happen. She might not be able to have a relationship with Harold, but she was determined to have one with Wade.

The next few weeks were hard for her. She wasn't worried that there weren't two Wades this time but worried whether anyone really loved her.

She cooked for Wade, yet he seemed preoccupied with school and his friends. Her sister Jenny hadn't visited with her for months. Pam attempted to call her, but she didn't return the call. Pam felt as though Wade was the only person that she had contact with.

It was late in the morning when Pam took the whole bottle of Risperdal pills. She hadn't planned on taking them; it was just something she did. She thought her family would be better off without her. She had brought them trouble and heartache. Pam told herself that she didn't want to live anymore as she swallowed the pills. She lay for what seemed like a couple of hours before she became scared and decided that the pills weren't going to put her to sleep. She only became agitated and restless.

She called the dispatch and told them what she had done. They immediately sent an ambulance to aid her. She was taken to the Berea hospital where they gave her charcoal to drink to counteract the pills. Her Aunt Freda showed up at the hospital. Her landlord had called Freda and told her what she'd done. Pam was glad that Freda was there. She needed her family to visit with. The doctor told her and Freda that she was free to go. He told her to see someone at Comprehensive Care that week. She told him that she would. Freda's son Harry drove them to Freda's house. It was clear to her that her cousin didn't want anything to do with her. She was sick. How could everyone ignore her because of this? She helped her family when they needed help? Why wouldn't her family have anything to do with her?

Freda asked Pam if she wanted to spend the night. Pam told her that she did. She didn't call Wade or try to reach him. He was too young to try and deal with a mother who had tried to commit suicide twice. She came to the realization that if she loved Wade she wouldn't bother him with her downfalls.

Freda dropped Pam off at her apartment the next morning. She tried to get Pam to stay with her for a couple of weeks, but Pam decided it wouldn't be for the best. Pam picked up the telephone and called Comprehensive Care to make an appointment with her therapist. She would have to spend only a few lonely, sleepless nights there. She was going to ask her therapist to send her to a personal care home for the mentally ill. She decided she couldn't be alone if she was going to cause harm to herself, It was only harming her and Wade. Really the rest of her family didn't care.

Pam kept her appointment with Mr. Harris the following day. She went to see him in the morning. She wasn't on any medicine at the time. Mr. Harris prescribed Seroquel to hold her over until he could get her into Raven House. Raven House was a stabilization unit for the mentally ill. Pam asked him if there was a Rehabilitation Center or personal care home that she could check herself into. She told him she was still sick and needed to be watched and treated for months or years. He didn't want to refer her to one of these places but agreed to do so while she waited in Raven House. He could tell that she needed much care or he wouldn't have agreed to help her. This was on a Friday. He sent her to Raven House that evening. Jenny didn't work on Fridays so it was convenient for her to take Pam to Raven House. Raven House was a small place. It had only seven or eight bedrooms, one bathroom and a dayroom with a television. There was a kitchen there where the attendants and patients prepared the food daily. They were served three meals a day along with nightly snacks. Pam lay in her room as thoughts and voices rang through her head. She'd never learned to use therapy techniques to make them go away. She'd always depended on the medicine to do this for her. She knew there was no way she could rest on the Seroquel. Dr. Stover had tried it on her once before. She told the nurse practitioner this the next day. The nurse increased the dosage and told her to try and relax until the medicine had time to take affect. It only caused her to pace back and forth and not be able to rest. Mr. Harris called her frequently to reassure her that he was working on getting her into Saint James Rehabilitation Complex. It was a rehabilitation center and personal care home combined. Pam was anxious to go as she saw that she couldn't live alone for much longer. He said he had talked with her sister and that she really didn't want Pam to go there. He only agreed to send her there because that was what she wanted. Pam told Jenny that she was too scared to live alone. She didn't even remember if she took her medicine the right way. Pam told Mr. Harris she would be better off in a place where they could help her with her daily living skills.

After about fourteen days she found out that Saint James Rehabilitation Complex had accepted her. She was thrilled. She would finally be going to a place where she could get help. They had nurses and a psychiatrist on staff there at all times. Her retirement papers could be filled out on site each year. Raven House was to transport her there the next day. It was only a couple of hours away from where she was at. It would be a two and a half hour drive for her family to visit her. She didn't know for sure that they would visit; she would somehow talk them into it. It was important for her to keep in touch with Wade, Harold and Jenny. Pam's first six weeks at Saint James went by quickly as thoughts rushed through her head. She played games such as certain colors meant that Wade had something to do with what someone else wore. Other colors meant Mr. Harris had sent that apparel for someone to wear. These games weren't healthy but they made time pass more quickly. She told the psychiatrist, Dr. Wise, of her games. Dr. Wise switched Pam from Seroquel to Lithium. He gave her the Lithium twice daily. Pam's blood sugar levels went down after she began taking the Lithium. The pacing continued each night, so Dr. Wise gave her Ambien to make her sleep. The psychotic games stopped, but the restless nights continued. Pam became involved in their work program. She began working at Saint James Creations. There she weaved rugs. She received about seventy dollars a week for her work. Pam found it hard to ride to work as she couldn't be still. The medicine didn't take care of her poor concentration and restlessness. She wished she could just sleep three out of seven nights a week. Dr. Wise seemed not to believe that she couldn't sleep. It was charted that she was up all through the night, wasn't it? She began to feel that Saint James was failing her. She still wasn't stabilized. Pam became so fatigued that she napped and slept when she could. It became a way of life for her to catch thirty minutes here and thirty minutes there.

After about two months at Saint James, Pam began to call her sister and son several times a week. She had enough money to purchase a phone card once a month. Jenny and Harold had divided her furniture when she left her apartment. Harold took some of the furniture while Jenny stored the rest. Pam didn't know that she had been so much trouble again. It didn't dawn on her that her apartment had to be cleaned out when she left. Jenny kept her car for when Wade turned sixteen. He could learn to drive with it or trade it in on a truck. Pam seemed to waste away at Saint James. It was an endless pace back and forth between outside and inside. Go out to smoke lay down a little while get back up and smoke again. The days passed by with this same pattern.

Pam soon became tired of weaving rugs, so she switched to the greenhouse to work. There they planted flowers and watered ferns. She spent three to four days a week doing this. It wasn't long until her first Christmas came around. Jenny came to pick her up. She spent the night with Jenny's family. Wade came to Jenny's to spend the night. This was the first Christmas night Pam had spent with Wade since Harold had left with him. It was exciting and fulfilling to watch him open the envelope of money she'd brought him. The bottle of perfume he gave her smelled good. It was Tommy Girl, one of her favorites. It was worth it to stay at Saint James if she could continue to visit with Wade at Christmas. She hadn't spent the night with her sister since college. She was glad Jenny cared enough about her to invite her. Pam dreaded the trip back to Saint James. It was about a three hour drive.

There wasn't much snow at Saint James Rehabilitation Complex that winter. It was cold but not so bad that you could sit outside for a little while. Pam enjoyed going to the movies and bowling. Saint James treated them about twice a month. Spring was just around the corner when she became interested in a man there named Steven. Steven was tall and brown headed. He wore a mustache. He was heavy built. Almost every male over there was a little overweight. The females were overweight too. Pam had gained a little weight but hadn't become too heavy yet. The medicine combined with three meals a day and two snack breaks seemed to cause everyone to be overweight. Steven asked Pam to visit with him at his parents. She liked getting away from the Rehab a little while, but he made her very nervous at his parent's house. He would throw his cigarette butts on the carpet and claim everyone was against him. Pam soon broke up with him because of his temper. She was afraid he might strike her. He soon left the rehab to live in an apartment. She didn't have much contact with him after that.

Spring was underway when Pam became irritated quite frequently at the greenhouse. She became agitated and snapped at things the supervisors said to her. One of the supervisors pulled Pam to the side and told her she should see Dr. Wise. Pam told her, "There are two of my sons and no one will believe me. I want the FBI to check this out and find both of them." I'll adopt Wade's look alike if they'll just put both them together. Pam's caseworker Linda told her that she would like for her to go to the hospital if she didn't see Dr. Wise. She agreed to see the doctor. The doctor put her on a couple medicines combined with her Lithium and Klonopin. Dr. Wise gave her Invega for psychosis and Trazadone for sleep. Klonopin was for nervousness and Lithium was supposed to stabilize her moods. Pam felt "doped" up, but it was needed for her to become stable. How could she ever live on her own while taking so much medicine? Her physical health was failing too. She took two kinds of cholesterol medicine and a thyroid pill. Pam felt as though she would never be able to live on her own again. She couldn't afford to keep up with all the medicine. It could be a constant visit to the doctor. Saint James was a medical facility, as well as a mental health rehabilitation complex. She knew after awhile that she would probably have to stay at St. James for a long time.

Pam didn't mind staying at Saint James Rehabilitation Complex. They took her to the movies, bowling, field trips and part time work. She'd made her mind up that as long as they let her participate in their activities and she got to go home for Christmas that she would stay put. This was the best place for her.

Pam's second Christmas was so much fun. She really liked to go home and see everything. The rehab took her home for Christmas. Pam's sister would bring her back Christmas evening. She got to see Wade, Jason and Jenny. Harold and she exchanged gifts in the car. She had been calling him consistently throughout the year. He had broken up with his girlfriend; Pam, deep down, wished he would take her back. She knew she could survive taking many medicines if he were interested in her again. He said that maybe next Christmas that she might be able to spend with them. She was looking forward to this. He always made sure he brought Wade to visit every two months. Pam didn't have as much money to give Wade because the government had cut back St. James work program. She hoped that next Christmas would be as good as this one. Life at Saint James continued to be relaxing. Everyone there was friendly and seemed genuinely concerned about the patients. They threw fun parties each holiday. The music and treats were delicious at their parties. The patients loved dancing under the black lights to the music. They had contests at their parties to make things more interesting. Saint James was a safe haven for the mentally ill. It had a long waiting list and it was hard to get in. Pam didn't want to lose her spot there unless her family wanted her to live with them. That spring after Pam's second Christmas a new patient moved into the personal care home. His name was Allen. Allen was young, black headed and brown eyed. He was very tall with a muscular build. Pam became infatuated with him the moment she laid eyes on him. Pam thought of how she hoped Harold would take her back. He showed an interest for awhile but later got back together with his girlfriend. Allen paid attention to her and she liked this. They became very good friends. At times he would talk sweetly to her, and at times he would ignore her for no reason. She often thought their age difference is what kept him from going with her. He would invite her on walks to the park. They would sit and swing for hours. One night while they were swinging he asked her if she would be his girlfriend. Pam said "Aren't I a little old for you? I'm old enough to be your mother." He said he was of age and he wanted to be more than just friends with her. Pam believed him and agreed to go with him as long as long as he didn't feel that she was too old. They spent the days walking, laughing, and going to work and parties. It made time pass much more quickly to have someone to go through the days with you. Pam was happy. Then to Pam's dismay Allen left to go and live with his family. Pam was heartbroken once more, but she soon got over it as the days ahead promised her Christmas.

This would be Pam's third Christmas at Saint James. She was looking forward to it because she'd learned that Harold was broke up with his girlfriend again. He wanted her to come and spend the week with him and Wade. She gladly let Saint James drop her off at his house for Christmas. Pam was fortunate that things well while she was there. He actually would discuss getting back together with her. She only knew that she had a hard time keeping up with her medicine while she visited through Christmas. She thought it might be because she was feeling anxious at his house. She had a hard time even when she stayed with Jenny one night. Nobody helped her with the medicine, but she wondered if she was taking it the right way. Mentally ill people have to take their medicines at the right time for it to work well. Christmas was soon over. It was up in the air to whether Harold had decided to take her back. He thought she was better but didn't know if she was ready for the real world. He had kept her wondering and hoping for the best.

Later that winter Allen returned to Saint James. They were friends but not close like they had been before he left. Harold got back with his girlfriend again and was to marry in the late spring. Everything was upsetting to Pam but she knew there would be better days and she had to make the best of things. She later that spring got a call from Jenny who told her that Freda had passed away. She was getting old as she was in her late eighties. She died of cancer. Pam had begun working at a steakhouse part time the week before the phone call. The steakhouse let her off for a day, so she could attend the funeral. It wasn't a large funeral, but most of the immediate family was there. Wade met Pam at the funeral home. Wade was a little hurt that he and Jason weren't asked to be pallbearers by Freda's son. He was nice but didn't go out of his way to be friendly. Pam talked with many family members while she was there. She told them that Saint James had been telling her for a couple of months that she was ready to be discharged. She wanted to live with some of the family. She told them that she had lived at Saint James so long that she was afraid to get totally out on her own. The family sympathized with her all but one. One of her cousin's wives made the comment that she was right where she needed to be. Pam always loved her so much, why would she make such a comment? Pam wished she hadn't talked to her at the funeral. Saint James waited patiently while she rode around with Wade for awhile. After about five hours they left to go back to Saint James. Pam always delighted in the ride to and from home.

Back at Saint James Pam became more involve with her work at the steakhouse. She began to work more hours. Saint James wanted to cut her days back to four days a week rather than six days a week. She went along with this. Gas prices had made the ride to work too costly. Soon one of the mangers at work named Anita wanted Pam to move in with her and her husband. Pam decided she would. She could work at the steakhouse and make extra money for herself and Wade. Anita picked Pam up at Saint James. She left her home that was safe, to go off with a stranger that she really didn't know. Anita kept barrowing money from Pam. She needed money for different things. Pam loaned her around fifteen hundred dollars. Pam noticed some of her Klonopin pills were missing. She found out that Anita's husband was a drug addict. Someone at work said he took pills without a doctor's prescription every chance he got. Pam wanted to move away from Anita. The other manager from the steakhouse, Bill, helped her find a furnished apartment. He gave her rides to and from work. Bill's car broke down so he asked Pam to lend him five hundred dollars. He promised to pay her back. Soon Pam was going to be out of money if she didn't say no to them. Part of Pam's medicine was missing. She didn't know what she'd done with it. Pam began having racing thoughts. The thoughts of two Wades and suicide played tricks with her head. She was all alone in a crisis situation. There was very little food in the house. She had very little money and no medicine hardly. What was she going to do? Pam picked up the phone and called Saint James. They sent her old caseworker, Linda, and another woman to help her. They took her to Comprehensive Care to be evaluated. They left her alone there with a few of her clothes. Comprehensive Care drove her to a crisis center in Jackson. This was about an hour and fifteen minute drive from Comprehensive Care.

The crisis center was a nice clean place that was newly built. Pam felt comfortable there but they told her she couldn't stay there for longer than seven days. They kept trying to convince her to go back to her apartment and work with a caseworker to manage her bills and medicine. Pam didn't want to go back and be alone. She was afraid she couldn't keep up with her daily living skills. Pam wanted to go back to Saint James. The crisis center called Saint James and asked if she could return there. Saint James told them that they couldn't take her back because they had all their beds filled. The people at Saint James noticed she wasn't sleeping so the doctor increased some of her medicine. This didn't work; she still didn't sleep. The crisis center was a cold place to be. They told her they were going to take her to a homeless shelter if she didn't go back to her apartment. Pam tried to explain to them she was too sick mentally to go to an apartment alone. Harold and Wade came to visit her. Both told them that Pam had tried to live alone but couldn't. Each time she tried to live alone, she would take an overdose of pills. They left hoping the crisis center would find some kind of placement for her. It came down to Pam's sixth day at the center. She was just allowed to spend seven days there. The supervisor at the center said she would try and find a placement for her. She was willing to help Pam find a safe place to go. The supervisor found a personal care home in Lexington, Kentucky. The name of this home was Grassy Personal Care Home. Pam agreed to go there. It would be closer to her family than Saint James. She hoped it was a good place. Pam was just glad that she didn't have to live alone. The crisis center called her sister Jenny and asked if she could transport her there. Jenny told them she would be there the next day at twelve noon. Pam was relieved and so was the center.

Jenny arrived at the crisis center around noon. Jenny was so pretty. Her hair was blonde and she was tall and slender. She had kept herself looking good over the years. Pam felt old beside her. Pam's hair was mingled gray now. She weighed more than she ever did. She wasn't what you'd call obese, but she wasn't slender like her sister. Pam had depended on Jenny to help several times. She always came to her aid. Wade was only eighteen and didn't know the way to these places. He wasn't experienced in following roads maps. He was just too young to take on the responsibility of helping with his mother. Jenny planned on staying all night in a hotel. Pam's restlessness made their stay at the hotel a miserable one. They arrived at Grassy Personal Care Home around ten o'clock the following morning. It was an old building. It was unlike Saint James. Pam wanted to tell Jenny she was going to have to stay, that she couldn't live with her. Grassy said that they would take her that day if she'd go and get her physical. Pam and Jenny returned with the papers from the physical. Grassy Personal Care Home admitted her that same afternoon. She didn't want to be on the street, so she was going to have to accept being in Grassy.

Chapter 10

The staff at Grassy Personal Care Home was friendly but the patients were different than any other people she'd had lived with before. All the women shared the same bathroom. The women were separated from the men. Many of them were sicker than Pam and unfriendly. They seemed absorbed into their own little world. Pam had a room with two other patients. The first week at Grassy was extremely hard. Pam was trying to adjust to her medicine and a new place at the same time. She slept just about day and night. Grassy was strict with their rules. They based their whole day on a point system. You get points for things like going to groups, bathing, washing hands, brushing your teeth, and cleaning your room. Pam raised her points to buy cigarettes and soda. She soon learned the ropes. This personal care home would cost her more because they hadn't started her in a work program yet. She didn't know if they had one or not, but she was going to ask her team leader. Pam was used to giving Wade a little money along for gas or clothes. She didn't think she would be able to afford this at Grassy. Grassy served three meals a day and a night time snack. Pam was on the diet menu since she had high cholesterol. The food was usually baked and low fat. Grassy didn't take you on as many trips as Saint James did. Saint James also bought clothes for their patients twice a year. Grassy expected you to buy your own clothes on practically nothing. Pam wanted to go back to Saint James even if it were farther away. She did talk with Grassy about trying to get back to Saint James. They wanted her to give them a chance for a little while longer.

Pam was thrilled to see Harold and Wade walking up the dusty hallway. She was so glad they'd come to visit her after only a month at Saint James. They talked and had a good time on their visit. They took her to a pizza place to eat. Pam talked to Wade and told him that she wanted him to apply at E.K.U. for a scholarship. She told him that this would save him money. Wade seemed to listen. Pam hoped he would do this. She spoke to Harold about making out a will. He had remarried, and Pam wanted him to make out a will so Wade would be included in the event of his death. Harold always lived for the moment. He said his wife wouldn't just take Wade's half, that she was a honest person. Pam told him she had used practically all of his money for a new house, hadn't she? Wade will be left with nothing if he should die. He agreed that he would make a will. Deep down Pam knew he wouldn't do this. She feared that he was a little too trusting of his new wife. Pam kissed Wade's cheek before they climbed into the black truck to drive away. She waved at them as though she might not ever see them again. She wished Wade would become more interested in learning the way to different places so he could go on his own. He carried a cell phone with him just about all the time. He could use the phone to call in case he broke down. Maybe he would soon grow up and take on a little more responsibility.

Pam got to know the patients more as the weeks followed. She hoped that they would make friends with her enough that they would teach her how to get around in Lexington. Saint James always took them shopping while Grassy expected them to ride the bus and go places on their own.

Her roommate Sarah was giving her problems already. She would turn the radio on late in the night and wake Pam and her other roommate Angel up. Sarah would open and close her dresser drawers loudly as she rummaged through them during the night. Theses things would awaken Pam. Grassy had strict rules on keeping things quiet at bedtime. Pam would get up and tell staff members what Sarah was doing to keep her awake. Sarah told the staff that Pam was a rat. Pam didn't appreciate this and told Sarah, "Stop calling me a rat! You're the one keeping everyone awake all night." Pam told her she wasn't going to bicker back and forth. Sarah told her she was worse than a rat. Pam became afraid and told staff. They didn't do much of anything; they only had a meeting between her and Sarah. Sarah didn't apologize; she only stated that she would have to leave her radio off. Was Sarah mean enough to choke her in her sleep? Pam worried about this. She wished she was back at Saint James rooming with Becky. They would never put up with someone threatening to kill another person. Pam had a hard time sleeping anyway. Her legs were restless during the night. Doctor Grant gave her medicine for restless legs syndrome. The medicine was the lesser dose. Pam needed the full amount to be able to settle down. She couldn't convince the doctor of this. At Saint James they gave her a strong enough dose to stop the restlessness.

Pam called Jenny a couple to three weeks after Harold and Wade visited her. She wanted Jenny to come and see her because she was lonely to see the family. Jenny agreed to come and visit on Saturday. Pam asked her to bring Wade with her if she could. Pam called Wade on a Thursday evening and told him Jenny was coming for a visit. Wade told her he would try to get up with Jenny to see if he could come with her. Pam looked forward to seeing them both on Saturday. Pam sat down in the library to talk with some of the other patients. The other patients talked about Obama and how they thought he might win the election. McCain wasn't mentioned.

They were having small talk about the news. One patient talked about why she was admitted to Grassy. She said it was court ordered for her to be there. Pam referred to them as patients because she hadn't learned everyone's names yet. Pam was still her own guardian. She hadn't been court ordered anywhere. She only knew that when she wasn't thinking straight, she couldn't live alone. She suspected many of the patients were like her that they had trouble living by themselves too. She had something in common with many of them. Pam sat Friday hoping Wade would be able to visit with Jenny. She thought about what she'd wear to look presentable to them. She had mostly T-shirts and jeans. These were the only thing she could afford on her budget. She was worried about buying clothes. She was afraid it would get to where she couldn't afford anything to wear. Pam had become lost in her thoughts again. She wasn't hearing what the other patients were telling her. Pam became frustrated that she couldn't follow along with the conversation and went to the dayroom to get her four o'clock medicine. She may have needed the medicine because after she took it she began talking to other patients again. One of the team leaders told her she wasn't socializing enough and needed to try to interact with other patients more. Pam thought the time at Grassy passed slowly. It was back and forth from the smoke area to her room that evening. She was soon going to run out of cigarettes as she had gotten only one pack with her points. She and some of the patients sat around in a circle and talked about music and other things. Some of them were afraid they'd have to stay there the rest of their lives. She told them she had to have someone to live with because she'd overdosed twice. She was frightened that she might overdose again. Some of the patients could identify with this because they said they'd overdosed on their medicine, drugs or alcohol. Pam returned back to her room to rest before dinner. She'd been fairly active that day, attending groups, talking with other patients and bathing. She'd managed to take a small nap too.

It had drizzled rain most of the day. It was the beginning of September and had been very dry and hot. The leaves on the trees were turning brown and yellow. The brown leaves had already begun to drop from the trees. They crunched under Pam's feet as she walked through the straw-like grass. Pam came in from outside to call Harold to tell him that Wade wanted to come and visit her with Jenny. She finally reached him on his cell phone. Pam asked, "Harold, will you make sure that Jenny knows that Wade wants to come and visit with me tomorrow?" He said, "I'll try and get up with her." Wade often said he would do something but never really followed through. He needed to try and see to things more on his own. Pam walked back to her room to lie down while she waited for dinner. As she walked past the attendants counter she noticed the clock read four fifty five. It would be dinner in about five minutes. She knew she wouldn't have time to lie down. She just walked back to the library and sat to wait for dinner. Soon it came over the intercom that dinner was being served. Everyone jumped up to race down to the basement. The stairs often reminded her of the stairs that she'd walked down at her and Harold's first home they built. Tears welled up in her eyes. Look where she was at now. These weren't the wooden stairs from her home, but the stairs made of cement in an institution. She longed for any stairs but these. As a girl she used to go down the stairs at Aunt Freda's to watch television. She used to enjoy watching Dark Shadows and Guiding Light. Jenny enjoyed more programs that were sitcoms. They never really fought over the television because the programs they liked were on at different times. Pam's basement at Aunt Freda's had a hard cemented floor covered with a braided rug. There was a big orange couch which was relaxing and warm to be on. There was a bookcase filled with books about romance, factual things and cartoons. Pam knew all the books covers and contents so well that she could almost quote the pages. She stopped thinking about the past when she heard the cook ask her if she wanted green beans too. She reached for a skim milk. The food at Grassy was nourishing and tasty most of the time. Pam ate what was on the dieters menu. Her cholesterol was too high for her to be on a regular diet.

Pam went outside after the meal to smoke. While she was there she didn't enjoy her company too well. There was a woman there that Pam found repulsive. She had her pants pulled up around her knees and had her smelly feet lying across the top of the picnic table. This was where most of the patients set their cigarettes and drinks. She didn't listen to what anyone had to say except herself. She went on how she was going to go to college and how smart she was. The woman was about fifty-five years old. Pam knew she was sick but couldn't understand why she didn't have better manners. Pam soon left the circle to go read or work in the library on the computer. She had an hour to wait until it would be time for her seven o'clock group. It was hard to find things to fill up her time. She most often ended up lying on her bed thinking about things from the past. Many of the people at Grassy couldn't carry on a conversation for more than four and five minutes. Most of them paced all day from room to room, Pam included. She wished she had something to do.

Pam was interrupted during her pacing by her seven o'clock "Positive Thinking" group. As she walked down the tiled hallway, Pam wondered if there would be participation in the group or if everyone would sit and listen to someone read to them. She dreaded the group because her legs were bothering her. The doctor really needed to increases her dosage of the medicine Requip. He had let her go for six weeks like this. He should believe her and increase the dosage. This was clearly negligence of patient care. Pam was five minutes late for the group. The attendant allowed her to stay and participate. She asked each person what their goal was. Pam told her that her goal was for her to keep her family close so they would agree for her to live with them. Other people in the group wanted to complete the program so that they could live on their own. Pam asked, "Can you stay here longer than the two year program?" The attendant replied "Yes you can live here as long as you feel you need to stay." With that answer the group was soon over.

Pam returned to her smoking partners outside. One of the patients asked her if she was going to get a snack. She told them that she was, and with that answer, she got up to go back upstairs. As she waited in line, she wished she could have been first. She scooted along against the wall while they took one person at a time. Pam went outside and ate her animal crackers. As she ate she thought back how she used to give Wade animal crackers when he was just small. He chewed on them as Pam waited anxiously for his first tooth to pop through the gums. Pam's train of thought was interrupted by another patient asking her if she was about finished eating her snack, she said she was but had to go back upstairs to take her medicine. She had learned to take her medicine on time. She didn't want to go a night without it. It seemed to make her mind rest. Although she still had a hard time settling down, she did get some relief part of the night. At nine o'clock Pam did her p.m. care to get ready for the night. All she knew was she hoped the days nap wouldn't disrupt her sleep. Pam said a short prayer as she began to lay down that night. She prayed that Jenny and Wade would have a safe trip the following day.

Pam awakened that morning to the voice of one of the male attendants telling her it was time for breakfast. She lay in the bed for about thirty more minutes. She wasn't very hungry, so she missed breakfast. She got up at eight o'clock and showered. She just remembered her sister was supposed to come and see her that day. She waited for her medicine patiently and wondered if what she had on would be presentable to her sister. As she sat there and waited, she told the attendant her roommate Sarah hadn't had a shower since Pam had come. She had been there somewhere around six weeks. The attendant said they'd take care of Sarah, for her to take care of herself.

The attendant was very rude and acted as if she didn't want to know that Sarah hadn't bathed. It dawned on Pam that they didn't care if Sarah had bathed or not. Pam had waited and waited for her medicine. If the nurse didn't get to her, she would miss morning store. Pam wouldn't have any cigarettes to smoke for that day if the nurse didn't hurry. She began to think the nurse didn't care about her or anyone else. She didn't mind that people missed their store. She would only say, "You need to get on the list sooner." Pam couldn't get on the list any sooner. The nurse told them to be on the list by 8 o'clock.

Pam was sitting in the dayroom thinking about a dream she was having when she awakened from her sleep. It was about how her cousin Harry and his wife turned her down when she asked if she could come and stay with them. She told them if she didn't get in a personal care home that she was going to be homeless. Harry didn't care. He told her they couldn't let her live with them and hung up on her. She wondered if Jenny would do the same thing if it came down to it. Pam was deep in thought when they called another girl's name to come and take her medicine. Pam was tired of waiting. She hoped she would get to the store on time to get what she needed that day. Grassy charged their patients too much for each item in the store. It was almost impossible to get enough points for a pack of cigarettes and a phone call both. Tears rolled down Pam's cheek as the clock read nine fifteen. She had missed store. She told the attendant that she hadn't left the dayroom since eight o'clock. She felt that it would be unfair if she didn't get to go to the store. They opened store back up again. She was able to get her drink and cigarettes. Pam went down the stairs to the outside booth. She noticed that it had rained the night before. She wondered if it had rained in Jackson County. As she sat down next to some of the other patients she noticed how friendly they were. One of them, Brandon, talked about how he had quit smoking. He said he felt as though his body was becoming cleansed of toxins. Pam said she could identify with that because she had quit smoking herself before. She told him that she liked his Levi jacket. It was unusual. There were pockets sewn all over its front and its back. She talked with him for awhile and then spotted crickets crawling all over the pavement in the smoking booth. She got an eerie feeling and told him she was going back upstairs to read for a little while. Pam hadn't really read for a long time. She wrote in a journal each day. She didn't want the patients to know that she wrote about her thoughts and conversations with them. She didn't want anyone to feel uncomfortable. It helped her to jot down little things throughout the day.

Pam waited anxiously in her room for the nurse to call her. She had a sore toe again. She'd had trouble with the toe for the last couple of months. Pam had seen a podiatrist earlier that month. She told Pam to keep her nail cut back, that she had an ingrown toenail. Pam tried doing as she said, but the nail seemed to become sore at the very sight of shoes. The nurse was going to look at the toenail to see if it needed clipping. Pam knew there would be pain involved because the toe was already sore. The nurse came to Pam's door and asked her if she would like to soak the nail before she attempted to clip it. The warm water felt good against Pam's toe. The nurse looked at her toe and said it was a little discolored around the nail. She said it would be hard for her to clip the nail since it was growing downward. She decided to clip it anyway. She also was going to make an appointment with the podiatrist. The podiatrist had told Pam if the toe remained sore, she would have to cut out the ingrown nail. Pam knew this would be very painful and didn't want to go through with the procedure. Pam was through soaking her foot and got up to go downstairs to smoke. She smoked quickly as it was nearing time for lunch. Thoughts of Jenny and Wade raced through her head. She remembered how Wade used to take a cigarette out of her hand and crumble it up to let it fall to the ground. He hated cigarettes and cigarette smoke. Jenny wouldn't let anyone smoke in her vehicle. She hated cigarettes too. Both of them just about went overboard when it came to cigarette smoke. Pam hoped they would come to see her before too long. She could hardly occupy herself until they got there. She waited for lunch. She was really hungry because she missed breakfast. They were having cheeseburgers for lunch. Pam wished they would have lasagna more often. That was one meal she really liked. Maybe Jenny would take her out to eat later that day. She hoped she would take her to an Italian restaurant. Pam had saved thirty dollars up for her and Wade to eat with. Pam's thoughts were getting on her nerves, so she got up from the chair in the dayroom to go to the library and wait for lunch. She could talk with some of the other patients while she was there. It would take her mind off of things.

Pam returned from lunch and went downstairs to the smoking booth. There were a few patients there smoking. They chatted about the lunch. They wished they could have real hamburgers rather than hamburgers made from soybeans. Pam grew tired of their conversation and went back upstairs to lie down. She woke to the sound of the nurse's voice. She wanted her to look at her toe. Pam got up from the bed and walked into the dayroom where the nurse looked at her toe. She said she thought it was infected. So she put some antibiotic ointment on it. Later Pam went to smoke again and wait for Wade and Jenny. It got to be one thirty so she went to call them. Jenny answered the phone. She told Pam that she would be over that evening, but Wade wouldn't be coming with her. He had a golf meet. Pam really wanted to see both of them. There were many obstacles that kept her from seeing her son. Pam wished they could spend the night together.

Even though they didn't talk for long periods they still had their own way of communicating together. Pam went to the midday café. There she enjoyed raspberry water. There were only one or two patients there. They talked with her about the day. The sun had peeked through the rain clouds. It was beginning to warm up outside a little. It reminded her of the days she spent under the shade tree at Freda's. There was a small picnic table there. Freda used it to serve Kool-Aid to Pam and her sisters. Rita stayed with their Uncle Bobby through the school year. They always were glad to have Rita for the summer. It was the best Freda could do; she had to separate one of the girls from the other two. Rita was younger and hard to keep up with so she went to live with another aunt and uncle. Rita loved her uncle and aunt so she stayed with them rather than switch back with Pam and Jenny. Pam, Jenny and Rita had been with these uncles and aunts since they were about two or three years old. There was only about one to two years difference in the girl's ages. Pam was so absorbed in her thoughts that she didn't notice the other patients had left the Midday Café. She quickly got herself up and rushed to her room. There she found her two roommates engrossed in music from the eighties. The radio stayed on most of the entire day. Pam got tired of listening to it so much. It was hard to take a nap with the radio constantly on. Pam would often lay down on the tiny half bed to think about what she wanted to journal about. The radio distracted her from this. She wished she had a different roommate.

The smoking circle was filled with patients. Everyone seemed to be enjoying the cooler air after the morning's drizzle of rain. It was getting closer to dinner time when Pam decided to join them. Her sister hadn't arrived yet. She knew that she was going to get there too late to take her to an Italian restaurant. While she was sitting there talking, she heard one of the attendants call for dinner. They all got up quickly to go down to the basement to dine on chicken and rice. The meal was nourishing and filling. Pam came back up to the dayroom around five thirty; she looked at the clock and headed back outside to the smokers booth. There she found a stick with an inch worm on it too play with. She talked with Donna as she played with the stick. Donna would laugh and say the inchworm was going up and then down on the stick. Pam glanced over and saw Jenny driving down the parking lot. She ran over to her sister's truck and said, "You have finally gotten here." Jenny told her that she'd brought Jason and Melvin to the ball game while they visited. Pam was disappointed that Wade wasn't with her. She told Pam that Wade wanted to come, but he had to play golf with his teammates. Pam left Jenny sitting in her truck while she went in to check out and get her purse. This reminded her of when Jenny got her first car. Pam would wait at the front door at school for Jenny to pull around in her car. Pam later got her own car after Jenny went away to college. Pam's purse was in her locker. The attendant had to unlock the locker for her to get her purse. It took about fifteen minutes for Pam to get back out to the truck.

Jenny drove Pam to a store in a shopping center down the street. Pam liked shopping even though she didn't buy anything. She told Jenny she didn't have very much money, so she couldn't buy anything. She told Jenny that Grassy didn't buy any clothes for them, that she would have to bring some clothes sometime next year. Jenny said she would take her shopping for clothes when it came time. Pam hated having to depend on other people for clothes and things. She'd always bought her own things since she'd left Aunt Freda's at eighteen. Aunt Freda and her uncle never bought her and Jenny another thing once they left their home. Pam always felt a little resentment that they didn't get them anything for birthdays and Christmas anymore. Maybe they didn't have enough money. Pam was deep in thought when Jenny raised her voice and asked if she was alright. Pam apologized and asked Jenny where they were going next.

Arby's had the best roast beef sandwiches in Lexington. They were cheap and affordable. The fifty dollars Jenny had gotten for selling Pam's couch was coming in handy. She would try to save the rest of it to buy a phone card. Pam used phone cards to call her family a couple times a week. Soon it was a time to go back to Grassy. Pam was supposed to report back in by nine o'clock. She hugged and kissed Jenny goodbye. Jenny told her she would try and be back over before Christmas since Grassy was closer than Saint James. Pam called Wade when she got back into the building. The attendant said Wade had called and left her a message. He'd called to tell her why he wasn't with Jenny. Pam called him back. It was the golf that kept him from being able to visit. He said he would be over in a couple to three weeks with Harold. Pam told him she would be glad to see him again. He told her that they would try to go to the movies when he came to visit. Pam told him that she loved him and with that they gave each other a kiss over the phone and said "Goodbye." Pam's mind was at ease when she lay down to go to sleep that night. Her prayer was long as she lay and went over her day.

The morning sun shined through Grassy's windows. It was about eight thirty a.m. before Pam could wake up enough to climb out of bed. She barely made it in time for a.m. care. They received one hundred points for a.m. and p.m. care. She took her medicine around nine fifteen. Pam went back to bed after this, but didn't go to sleep. She lay and thought about the first day she ever went to church. She was about seven years old. She and Jenny would walk out to the little Christian Church down the road. Their neighbor, nicknamed Blue Jay, would walk with them. He always wore a black suit, black necktie, and black shoes. He wore a white button down shirt underneath his suit. Pam always wondered what his real name was. Blue Jay passed away when she was a teenager. She couldn't remember his funeral but she was sure his family had one for him. Maybe he was buried a long way away and she didn't get to go.

Pam lay in bed remembering when she was young, she fell asleep. One the attendants at Grassy woke her to say it was time for lunch, and that she had missed breakfast and had better eat a few bites. She dragged herself out of bed and walked down to the dining area. She wished they had left her in bed all day. After eating she went back upstairs to lie down again. This time she slept until two o'clock. An attendant came and woke her up from her sleep. It was Sunday and there wasn't anything else to do but sleep. She wished they would let her sleep since she was unable to sleep most of the time. She got out of bed and went outside to the smoking booth. Sandra was sitting out there waiting for someone to talk to. Pam sat down beside her. She asked Pam if she had been resting, and Pam told her that she had. Sandra told her the church she used to go to when she was a child had been torn down. Pam told her the Christian church she used to attend as a child was still there but used as a storage building. The people at the Christian church had built a new church. She and Wade had gone to a new church regularly when he was small. He was an angel in their Christmas play one year. Pam told Sandra it had been nice talking to her, that she was going back inside. Pam went back inside to the Library. The library was deserted. There wasn't anybody in there reading or working on the computer. Pam went in and sat down on one of its soft plastic chairs. It was hard for her to stay awake because she was still sleepy. Her medicine seemed to work much better during the day. Many people passed by the door as Pam sat there snoozing. One of the attendants told her that she was not allowed to sleep in the library. She became agitated at him, and told him she wasn't bothering anything. He told her to either find a book to read or get out of the library. She chose to leave the solitude of the library to go back outside. Pam sat outside with the group of smokers when the topic of suicide came up. The patients often talked about their experiences with suicide when they were sick. Pam felt uncomfortable because it made her think back when she was a teenager. She had tried to puncture the vein in her wrist with a sharp pen. She had dug into her wrist until there was countless scratch marks on it. No one knew about this because she wore long sleeves all winter long. Another time she tried to commit suicide by taking a whole bottle of aspirin. Pam couldn't remember why she took a whole bottle of aspirin. She could just remember getting them down and swallowing four or five pills at a time. Neither incident seemed to harm her in any way. So nobody really ever found out about it. Pam didn't tell the patients about her experience with suicide but became disturbed by them. She got up from the round table and told everyone that she would see them later. She went upstairs to the dayroom to watch television for awhile. Kentucky was playing football against someone on the television. She used to play pass with her cousins in the yard at Aunt Freda's. Pam had been exposed to sports all through her childhood. Her cousins were made up of mostly boys. Wade had mostly boys for his cousins too. His cousins were older than him, except for Jason and Rita's two girls. His cousins rarely visited him. Jason would stay up all night every now and then. Pam hoped Wade wasn't having any suicidal thoughts. She decided that she must have been sick during her teenage years but got better after she left for college. She couldn't remember having any suicidal thoughts during her college years.

This Sunday had been a boring day. Pam received no phone calls or made any phone calls. It had been a day of relaxation but yet disturbing. She had thoughts of many things that were troubling to her. She wished she could think of fun things rather than things that had to do with death. Why did she have to think at all? Why couldn't she just live from day to day? Hopefully Grassy will help her to live for the future rather than live for the past. It was hard to live for the future when her family was so far away. She was constantly afraid that she wouldn't have enough money to buy phone cards to call her family. Pam knew she had lived in poverty since her early retirement. She had thought of ways that she could make more money. All of them involved working for the school system. She couldn't do this because her disability retirement had very strict rules about working for the school system once you've left on disability retirement.

At Saint James they had a very good work program at one time. Pam was sure that they would try and build their program back up. Grassy didn't have much of a work program. She wouldn't be able to make any extra money. Would her family understand this and give her things? She didn't think so. While she sat in the dayroom her thoughts were very persistant, they kept darting from one thing to the next. She gave into them and began journaling. This was the only thing she knew to do. She wondered if her thoughts and ambitions were written down maybe someone would read them and have some ideas on how to help her. They would only tell her to keep them for her to make reference to. Pam decided she wasn't going to journal anymore. She decided to just start expressing her thoughts verbally. Maybe if she did this someone would have some suggestions for her on how to cope with her future and her past. Her Sunday was turning into a nightmare. Things went over and over in her head until they became jumbled together. She began writing her thoughts even more. She was educated and people that were educated loved to write and read. It was second nature for them to do this. If she read anything she became restless and would stray off into her own little world. Pam was becoming overwhelmed with her own self. How could she break these redundant episodes?

Pam got up from the dayroom to go outside. She began to talk to some of the patients about dinner. They were like her; they didn't like what was being served for dinner, so two or three of them went in together to order a pizza. They were supposed to bring the pizza within thirty minutes. Pam hadn't got to eat pizza since she'd been at Grassy. When she was at Saint James, they ordered pizza once weekly. They had extra money because they were in the work program. Pam could hardly wait. Her mouth watered for the taste of cheese and tomato sauce.

The coke machine upstairs charged seventy five cents for a soda. It used to cost fifty cents out of the machine. Soda would make the pizza even better. Pam usually got sprite because it didn't have caffeine in it. The caffeine tended to make her restless leg syndrome worse. She took medicine for it, but the medicine helped very little. The cost of living had even affected the patients in personal care homes. The pizza finally came. The group sat and enjoyed their pizza and soda while they listened to the radio. The radio sang, "If I Could Be Your Hero". This reminded her of Wade and Harold. How she wished she was sitting with them eating pizza and relishing in the cool breeze. The trees seemed to tower over them as they ate. Pam knew this was good times even though Wade and Harold weren't with her. They were probably having a good time cleaning around their new house. The weather in Kentucky was beautiful this evening. Pam wished she could sprout wings and fly in the smooth cool air. The songs on the radio sang about love and how this was the time of our lives. She knew that the war in the Middle East had put a damper on many people lives, but she thought of how its inhabitants would open their arms to the heavens when they were finally free. The economy had made life in the United States almost like a jail cell for many. The people here pondered through places that gave away free clothing and food. She had even felt as if she would be in that predicament in a few years.

The evening was coming to a close as Pam got up from the group to go and call Wade. She was ready to make her once weekly long distance phone call. She hoped he would be home. She hated to leave the group because she was enjoying the music. One song sang of misconceptions. The song really hit home to her as she walked away from the group.

When Pam got back upstairs she took a warm shower. It was relaxing to change into her pajamas early. After she took her shower, she used her free weekly long distance phone call to call Wade. He was home alone as usual. Harold had left to be with his wife. Pam could hardly get used to talking with just Wade. She felt like there was a void in her life since Harold had remarried. Wade talked about his golf and how it would be after golf season before they would be able to visit. Golf season would end somewhere around the first of October. Pam told him that it would be about five weeks before they would be over. He disagreed and said that it would be more like four. They talked about Wade applying for a full scholarship at E.K.U. This university was his choice to go to college. Pam had gone to E.K.U. to get her teaching degree. She also earned her fifth year at E.K.U. When she went to college, it was possible to earn a fifth year if you took a few more college classes. Pam remembered pulling her red Camaro into the parking lot at E.K.U. She walked a long way each day to get to classes. She was thin at that time and dressed in white shorts or white pants most of the time. She was asked out by some of the college freshmen. One was a man who she met in one of her classes. He wore long blonde hair, tight torn jeans, white tank top and construction boots. He offered to take her to a Rolling Stones concert. Instead, she bought the tickets. She and Harold went to the concert. She often thought of this man and wished she'd gone with him. Maybe things would have ended up differently. Wade has never been to a concert. Most teenagers his age have been to a concert. She and Harold never had enough money to spend on concerts. Wade was getting old enough to work part-time. He still has one more year in high school to go. He didn't seem to want to date yet. He liked girls. Pam noticed this in the things he said when he visited her. She thought Wade was somewhat quiet and he might be a little too shy to ask a girl out. He once made the comment to her that he wasn't attracted to any of the girls in Jackson County. There was plenty of time for him to find someone at college or where he would later work. It's important for Wade to find someone to share his life with. They kissed each other goodbye over the phone. Pam gave her point book to the attendants to take off twenty five points for the phone call. Pam wished she didn't smoke so she could save up more points.

The evening had been pleasant. Pam had enjoyed pizza and a nice conversation with Wade. She was ready for bed. She hoped she could go to sleep after napping so much in the earlier hours. She had trouble with sleep. If it wasn't restless leg syndrome, it was waking up to nightmares. Many times she just couldn't fall asleep. It didn't matter how many hours she sat up. She still couldn't fall asleep. She'd tried exercising vigorously in the early part of the day. Nothing seemed to work. Pam said her prayer that night. In it she thanked God for having the points to call Wade. She prayed that she would continue to have the money to buy phone cards. Her prayer seemed to worship material things a little. She thanked God anyway and lay down to go to sleep.

It was one o'clock when Pam got up to go to the bathroom. She hadn't been asleep yet. Her roommate kept getting up and staring at her through the curtain. She was going to ask her team leader if she could move in the morning. She hoped he would let her because Pam felt scared when her roommate did this in the middle of the night. Pam didn't wake up for breakfast that morning. She was so tired from being up all night that she couldn't bring herself to get out of bed. The attendant came back to her room at eight o'clock to see if she was alright. She told him she was tired from not sleeping the night before. Pam crawled out of bed slowly, and did her a.m. care. She went to the counter to get her notebook filled out and to take her medicine. Then she returned to her room to journal for a while.

Pam found out that her team leader had come in so she went to talk to him about her roommate. He told her that he didn't have any concerns about her roommate hurting anyone. He had never known of her to hurt a fly. Pam told him that she felt intimidated and she couldn't feel safe in the room alone with her. He said that unless she was actually saying or doing something to her, there wasn't anything he could do. Pam told him she didn't feel the same way about this situation. Her roommate was doing something by pulling the curtains back and staring at her. Pam remembered her threatening to kill her. She felt uneasy as she walked out of his office. The only other time she had ever been threatened was in the seventh and eighth grade. Diane Potter threatened to beat her up if she didn't stay out of her way. Pam hadn't done anything to be around her. She often wondered what she meant by staying out of her way. At nine-twenty Pam had a group in the activity room. Maybe this would take her mind off of things. She tried to attend group regularly because they got points for this. She needed all the points she could get for phone calls, soda and cigarettes. Pam wished she had some type of job to make extra money. Pam walked downstairs to the smoke group. There, the radio was playing. The song on the radio sang, "Don't bring me down." She immediately became sad and thought of how she'd just about brought Wade down with her sickness. How could she ever make it up to him? Nobody could replace time with actions and words that were lost. Pam wished she could go back in time and pitch those pills in the trash. She wasn't strong enough to make her racing thoughts and voices go away. She wasn't strong enough to keep up with the many medicines that kept her mind free. Wade saw her through a different picture than what she imagined. He seemed well adjusted over the phone and in person, but was he really? She hoped he would forgive her and try to make their visits with each other special ones. There might come a day when he became too busy in his life to visit with her. She was determined not to let her downfalls bring him down. It was for the best that she stayed away and visited when she got the chance. Maybe Wade would develop into a person who was strong and could say no to whims that passed before him. Pam became so involved with her thoughts that she missed her nine-twenty group. They told her just to come to Mind-benders on Tuesday to make it up. She tried to stay focused enough to attend the ten o'clock group. The groups really helped to take her mind off things that were bothersome. Games often brought these bothersome things out into the open.

Pam walked to the library. There she thought about what the smokers talked about while they sat and smoked. One lady told how she was in a facility that was covered with cockroaches. She said they were all over the floor and tables. The food in the facility was horrible. She said the patients drank powdered milk with their meals. Pam didn't want to have to go to a place like that. She hoped Wade would never have to lead this kind of life. The lady said at the time she didn't have any choice because she didn't want to be out on the street. Pam got up from the library chair to go to her ten o'clock group. There were only five of them in the group. The group was about politics. It discussed policies and beliefs within the Democratic and Republican parties. She listened as they compared the two parties. Pam had always been a Republican. Since she had become sick, Pam learned that many of the special programs that support the mentally ill are developed during the Democratic terms. Republicans believe that the poor people should be more responsible in supporting themselves. She felt that the Republican Party needed to show more compassion for the mentally ill. If it weren't for strong arms control, she would be a Democrat. She had voted for Republicans and Democrats before. Pam was a Clinton fan as well as a fan of Bush. Who would she vote for this fall? She was leaning towards the Democrats because of special programs for the mentally ill and a more universal healthcare system. She had seen and lived in sickness for the last eight or ten years, so she knew what it was like not to have anywhere to turn. Pam left the group with her mind made up to vote Democratic this time. She hoped they would keep the arms control up to pace in the United States. Pam headed toward the dayroom to sit and wait for lunch. She and another patient talked about her teaching career. She told her that she had taught second grade for eighteen and half a years. Pam really missed teaching. She wished she was in good enough health to go back to it. It would be like a fifty year-old woman just beginning her career all over. She couldn't take the chance of losing her disability. She felt fine most days but sometimes she had relapses with her illness. Soon they called for lunch over the intercom. She'd missed breakfast, so she ate a hardy lunch of turkey and dressing. Pam couldn't wait until dinner because they were having pizza.

As Pam walked down the hallway to her room one of the patients turned and yelled. "Stop trying to chop my head off!" Pam hadn't said anything to her. Why were these people so hard to get along with? Pam was very afraid of all of them. She went to her room only to find the lights on and the radio playing. There was no place here for her to enjoy quietness. It all was becoming too overwhelming for her to deal with. She wanted to go back to Saint James. Even there the residents were constantly at each others' throats. No one had verbally attached her there.

Pam waited for her fifty dollars each Monday. She stood in line and waited her turn. When she finally made it into the finance officer's office, she found out that she had two bills to pay. One was to the Urgent Treatment Center while the other was to Grassy. By the time she paid these two bills and got her fifty dollars, she had only two hundred dollars left. She got one of the men to show her how to ride the bus to a shopping center. Pam wanted to go there to purchase a phone card. It was kind of scary riding a bus to a place you're not familiar with. She didn't know when to pull the cord to make the bus stop. She wasn't aware of where she was at exactly. It was a good thing one of the patients went with her. She studied the road signs but still got turned around. What would anyone do if they got lost out by themselves? She had no idea how to get back to Grassy. Pam hoped Wade would never be faced with this dilemma. When she finally made it back to Grassy she learned that she'd got points for checking in and out. She would have to make sure someone went with her for a while. Her friend and she made it back in time for dinner. They were supposed to have pizza and salad that evening. Their meals were good at Grassy, but they often didn't give enough of what you liked. Pam went to the dayroom to wait for her medicine. After getting her medicine, Pam lay down on her bed to rest. It was seven fifteen when she woke up. She hoped this didn't interfere with her sleep later on that night. The store was getting ready to open, so Pam gathered up her point book. A soda out of Grassy's store was one hundred points. The smoking group outside awaited her, so she went outside to listen to the music and drink her soda. While she was there they talked about how a soda drink was a real luxury when they were children. Pam could remember getting only one soda a week until she was out of high school. They drank milk and water at her house. The milk was brought from a cow every two or three days. It was cheaper to buy it fresh from a cow than to buy it from the store. She felt old sitting there talking about things from her childhood. Pretty soon she got up to go back inside. It was time for her relaxation group. She usually liked going to this group. They practiced various relaxation techniques. It wouldn't be long until bedtime.

Pam woke up the next morning to the sounds of chattering voices. The attendants were talking to the patients very loudly. It was six forty-five when Pam looked at the clock. She was in a dream about her and Harold. They'd gone to a funeral and she wore a ball gown to the funeral home. People were staring at her and talking about how beautiful the gown was. It was white with little round colored beads all over it. The beads were a light tan. Harold's whole family was there. They kept trying to get him to dance with Pam. Pam's uncle Raymond had died. People were looking at him and then would come out into the lobby and watch her and Harold dance. Pam kept wishing she hadn't worn the gown because it was being disrespectful to her uncle. Her dream ended when she was awakened by the sounds of cheerful talking. Pam kept laying back down for a good fifteen minutes before she was fully awake. She got up to go smoke at seven o'clock. She smoked quietly outside by herself. It had rained the night before, so the air was cool and damp. There was a slight breeze blowing. It looked as if it was going to be cloudy the rest of the day. Pam hurried back upstairs to do her a.m. care. The attendant wanted her to change shirts. Pam told her she would change when she showered later that morning. After Pam got her a.m. care over with she took her medicine. The nurse looked at her feet and saw that Pam's big toe was infected around the nail. She gave Pam antibiotics and cream to rub on her toe. Pam would have to go back to the foot doctor.

At nine-twenty, Pam's groups began for that day. As she looked over the board she saw that she had four groups to attend. They were Good Morning Grassy, This Is Your Life, Mind Benders and Fun and Games. Pam looked forward to going to these groups because it made time pass more quickly. She wouldn't be able to shower until after dinner. The groups would fill up her morning. In the first group, Good Morning

Grassy, they talked about birthdays, horoscopes, a woman who had left her child in a van and famous people. The second group, Mind Benders, was more interesting. In it they actually played mind games. They worked with simple one digit and two digit math problems, colors, and word recall. She got all the math problems correct and got all the colors correct. She got fifteen out of twenty words correct. Her mind didn't wander through either one of these groups. The third group, This Is Your Life, brought up old memories of when she was a teenager. There she talked about how she got her driver's license when she was eighteen. Then they talked about their favorite music. Her favorite group was the Rolling Stones. She told everyone about how she went to see the Rolling Stones when she was in college. To this day Pam still loves the Stones. In the forth group, Fun and Games, they played hangman. The attendant would draw lines on the board for a word about September. They would go around the table calling off letters until someone got the word. Pam only got two words out of ten correct. Another woman named Carrie got the other eight words. Some of the players didn't get any words. Pam was happy with her two words. Pam couldn't concentrate during hangman because she kept thinking about Wade. She wondered why he hadn't been to the dentist. Wade's teeth were very important. It's Harold's job to see to his dental care. She didn't care if he was eighteen years old. He still needed his teeth cleaned a couple times a year. When she got out of group the first thing she asked Carolyn about was her teeth. She wanted to know when Grassy was going to take her to get her teeth cleaned. Carolyn told her that it would be sometime in October. Pam was constantly worrying over things. Doesn't a little bit of worrying make you go ahead and act on things? Pam returned to her room to get a cigarette. The cigarette would calm her down.

Pam decided she was going to call Harold and talk to him about getting Wade's teeth looked after. Maybe he would have Wade go to the dentist if she called. This was something that only she cared about. Harold had devoted his entire life to his new wife. He always made sure Wade went to the dentist before he was married. Pam stopped thinking this or thinking that. She just decided to go pick up the phone and call him. The phone rang four times before he answered. She called his cell phone. He was at school substitute teaching. She asked him if he could hear her. He seemed not to know who it was. She told him it was Pam. He acted glad to hear from her. They talked about Wade's teeth. Harold said he would be over in three to four weeks. Pam thanked him and told him goodbye.

Later that day Pam talked to Nancy her team leader about working at the greenhouse. Nancy told her that they would have to discuss it during staffing. Her staffing date wasn't until the following week. Pam hoped they would let her work at something because she was becoming easily bored. If she didn't have to take so much medicine, she would be alright on her own. The medicine was the tricky part to her illness. Pam walked out of the dayroom to go back outside. She sat there and smoked a cigarette. The building she lived in was close to the highway. She gazed at the traffic as it passed by her. At one time Pam couldn't stand the roar of cars and trucks. Now she was in a place where she couldn't get away from them. If she had to be confined somewhere why did it have to be next to a major highway? She should have never left Saint James. She had told the staff at Grassy several times that she wanted to go back to Saint James. Everyone just changed the subject and acted as if they couldn't hear her. Pam noticed the sky had grown even darker. The rain began to drop on her head and shoulder. It felt good to have the cool water trickle down her face. One of the patients yelled, "You'd better go in before you melt." She just laughed and replied, "Don't worry my skin isn't made of sugar!" She danced around in the rain as it wet her whole body. Her clothes were soaked as she made her way back up the stairs. When she got upstairs Pam, smiling, gathered up dry clothes and headed for the shower. The droplets of water that came out of the shower head were much more forceful than the rain. The water that came out of the shower was hot instead of cool. Pam slicked back her hair with her trembling hands as she remembered bathing with Harold from time to time. She let the bubbles from the soap cling to her body for a few minutes before she stood directly underneath the water. When she looked down the old cracked cement floor was covered with suds that once covered her body. She wished she was back in their brown brick home showering. This building would never fulfill her need to live in her nice, safe brick home. Pam returned to her room to put away her things. She quickly went out in the hall to show her toe to the nurse. It was swollen with a yellowish patch at the corner of her nail. The nurse gave her another antibiotic pill and said she was sending for some Epsom's Salt to soak her toe in.

It wasn't long until time for her Into the Garden group. It was four o'clock when she entered the glass doors to go to her group. They were asked to list things they thought gardening was beneficial for. She wrote down exercise, fresh food and to have a hobby. Then they measured the plants that they were growing. Pam had chosen daisies to grow. She liked daisies because of the rhyme says, "He Loves Me, He Loves Me Not." She chose daisies to put on her baby's grave. She hoped she would get to visit Jackson County soon and be able to go to her baby's grave. Harold and she usually went there together. She was lost in her thoughts when the attendant said they could go. She had earned another hundred points. Pam looked over her point book for that day. She had around seven hundred points added onto her already eleven thousand. This made her have a total of eleven thousand seven hundred points in her notebook. She felt as though she were back in school again. As she walked back down the hallway to her room she noticed it said four fifty on the clock. She went and put her point book back into her room.

She headed for the library to wait on dinner. When she got there Chris was sitting at the computer. He asked her if she would like to hear about his dream. She told him she would love to hear about his dream. He said, "I was dreaming about a woman and when I woke up my fingers smelled like a woman." Pam told him he had embarrassed her on purpose. She walked out of the library to the front of the staircase leading downstairs to the lunchroom. As she stood and stared at the door she wished she hadn't talked to Chris. He was acting like a school boy rather than a grown man. The men at Grassy had no manners. At Saint James she had found love again. She wished she could see and talk to her old boyfriend. He had never said anything like what Chris had just said. She waited patiently for them to call dinner. Dinner was fish, french-fries and coleslaw. Pam ate almost all of it. She wished she could turn down half of her meals. She didn't want to gain any more weight. Grassy served only three meals a day. It was hard to wait six hours without anything to eat.

After dinner Pam went back outside to sit in the chilly air. It wasn't so bad outside with her jacket on. She sat and looked at the cars pass by.

She counted as a red one and two white ones went by. As she counted she was interrupted by two of the patients that had come out to sit too. They were talking as they took draws from their cigarettes. Pam asked, "What are you all doing?" They asked if they could come and sit beside her. They talked for about five or ten minutes then went inside. It was an endless cycle at Grassy to go outside then back inside. It seemed as though everyone did it. Television was hard to watch there because the screens were so small. Many of the patients just sat in front of the television without really knowing what was going on. When Pam was a girl, she would sit for hours writing poems. She would look up words in a dictionary trying to find things that rhymed. She didn't know what happened to her pages of poetry. In this day and time kids and adults spent many hours in front of the television. She wished she could capture her creative moments when she was young. It might not physically help her, but it would do wonders for her mental state. Pam was growing tired and it was nearing time for her to go to bed. She decided to have one last cigarette before she went upstairs to go her p.m. care. The cigarette wasn't full strength. It was only a light, but it tasted strong. She needed to quit but they seemed to fill up time. She felt lost without her cigarettes. She was definitely hooked on them. There was a time when she used to sneak in the barn and smoke as a girl. Pam stopped doing it out of fear that she would get caught stealing cigarettes. She didn't pick them back up again until her late twenties. Then she quit when she was pregnant with her children. She didn't smoke while she was pregnant or after for a long time. Then her nervousness seemed to get her started back to smoking. She was proud that Wade had never started smoking. He had said no to alcohol and drugs. He seemed to be very clean cut. Pam thought about how he looked now. She couldn't understand why girls weren't falling all over him. He was tall and thin. His eyes were a sky blue. His teeth were white and straight. Wade's hair fell across the back of his neck in curls. His good looks were breath taking. Did they shy away from him because of his mother? Maybe he wasn't giving off enough signals to girls to let them know he was interested. Pam had worried herself to death about what Wade might be feeling. It was time to say her prayers and go to bed.

Chapter 11

The sound of the side door opening and closing woke Pam up. Then she heard someone yelling, "Breakfast!" She wasn't very hungry so she decided to roll over and go back to sleep. A dream had kept her from waking up completely. She was enjoying what she was doing in the dream. First she dreamed that she was in her classroom. The kids were cutting out Halloween characters to hang up in the room. Then they went from Halloween to house plans. They began to draw house plans. She was totally absorbed in these activities when she was awakened. She tried to go back to sleep, but the sounds in the hallway wouldn't let her. She just rolled out of bed to get dressed. Reaching for a cigarette Pam wondered who was outside. When she got down to the smoke booth the only person there was Jenkins. Jenkins asked her if she had another cigarette to spare. Pam told him she didn't have any extra ones. If you started giving one away you had to keep giving them away. Pam learned this very quickly at Saint James. If cigarettes were made more affordable this wouldn't happen. Pam smoked only half of her cigarette then went upstairs to the dayroom to wait for her medicine. There were six patients sitting in the dayroom. One was sitting and talking to herself while two were reading the paper and talking quietly. The other three were just sitting staring at the television. How could Pam cope with these patients day after day? An attendant came over to sit with them for awhile; he took notes on their behavior. Pam wondered what he was writing about her. Mamie the nurse came over and asked,

"How is your toe?" Pam answered, "My toe got worse and the other nurse had to call the doctor and put me on an antibiotic. I've been soaking it in Epsom Salt." Mamie replied, "I hope Denise sees to it this morning." Denise was one of the morning nurses. She was one of the nurses that Pam liked the most. Pam waited for the nurse to call her. In just a few minutes the nurse called her back to take her medicine. As she took her medicine the nurse looked at her toe. She said, "Are you ready to soak your foot?" Pam said, "I need to soak it for about fifteen or twenty minutes. It seems to be helping." The nurse told her the antibiotic was helping more than anything. Pam left the nurses station to go and get a pan to soak her foot in. After soaking her foot she went down to the smokers' booth to smoke. Chris came and sat beside her. She immediately got up and went upstairs. Pam had made her mind up that she wasn't going to have anything to do with Chris.

Pam came back to her room. The bed looked inviting. So she lay back down for a while. The hours crept by until lunch. It was cooks choice day. Lunch would probably be good today. Pam was extremely hungry because she had missed breakfast. She got out of bed to go back outside. Marie was sitting in the smokers' booth. "When are you coming back over to Grassy?" Pam asked. "It will be a couple of weeks before I'm discharged from the hospital." Marie answered. Marie had been taken to the hospital because she had been threatening the patients and staff. She told Pam that the staff wouldn't do anything when someone bothered her. She said that she drew social security and had ninety-one thousand dollars in the bank. Pam thought to herself if she had ninety-one thousand dollars how she wouldn't be at Grassy. Money was a problem for her. Teachers don't make enough money for the amount of education they have to get. Lunch was soon called so Marie and Pam went up to have fish, salsa and rice. The cooks hadn't chosen very good food to be served at lunch. Pam was disappointed they didn't have burritos instead of fish. She and Marie ate lunch and Pam returned to her room.

A little while after lunch the attendant came to Pam's room and told her that her clothes were dry in the laundry room. She had completely forgotten about washing her clothes that morning. She gathered up her things and took them back to her room to be folded and hung up. Soon after folding clothes Pam fell into a deep sleep. She napped until about two o'clock. She woke up from her nap wanting liver from Famous Recipe. If she had the money she would ride the bus to go get some. She began journaling to take her mind off of the hunger. When she was married and working if she wanted something to eat she prepared it or went out and bought it. Not having money was a pain. Street people live in hunger just about twenty-four hours a day. Her team leader later asked her if she would like to go to a play. She said if it were free she'd be interesting in going. She signed up for the play on the list hanging on the board. The play would fill up time and be good entertainment. Pam became so hungry that she decided to go out to Rally's and get a chili dog. This might hold her over until dinner. Walking next to the traffic was a big dread. Even though she didn't imagine cars were following her she still remembered the frightened feeling she had when she thought they were. Pam had a real problem with thinking things that weren't true. Rally's had tables and benches to eat at. These tables were outside. The traffic roared by as she sat and ate her chili dog. She just knew the people in the cars were staring at her. At least they weren't saying things to her as they drove by. Pam forgot to sign out when she left to walk out to Rally's. She soon finished her hot dog and walked back to Grassy. It was only about a ten minute walk.

Pam went back upstairs to the day room to get her medicine. She had complained earlier of how hard it was to have enough points to buy a pack of cigarettes. One of the attendants brought a list of things you could do in one day to earn points. It was an unrealistic list. Pam thought about telling her a head full but it would only make matters worse for her. Things in the store that they used their points to buy were priced too expensive. You had to give up this or that to buy something. Pam still wished she was back at Saint James. At Saint James they paid their patients money to work. There you could earn enough money to buy things each week. Pam had sat for what seemed like an hour waiting for her medicine. The nurse was in no hurry to give her medicine. This was a very rude place. The staff was very short with the patients. Pam decided she was stuck. The staff at Saint James was never consciously hateful or short with the patients. The people in Grassy and Saint James were very sick. Why didn't the staff see that? The nurse finally called Pam back to take her medicine. She wasn't friendly and seemed matter of fact about things. Pam had trouble with this same nurse before. The nurse was old and had worked at Grassy for many years. There was an air about her that seemed to twist things around to get her way. Pam wished she could tell her a head full, too.

They called dinner. The menu said fish again. This was the third time in a row that they'd had fish in two days. Pam wasn't very hungry but decided she would eat since it would be a long time until breakfast. If a person missed a meal around here they would just go hungry until the next meal. If you're at your own home you can eat when you want. These places should have more snacks for its patients. The tables were almost full when Pam entered the cafeteria. They were having Salisbury steak. It looked terrible. The meat was all soggy and soft. She only ate a few bites of steak and corn. She got up from the table disgusted at the food. School lunches were better than this.

At seven o'clock it would be time to leave for the play. Pam couldn't wait to get out for a little while. She went outside and sat with some of her friends. They weren't really friends; just acquaintances. They sat and talked about the play. Some of them had gone to plays before. This would be the first play that Pam had attended in years. She used to take her classroom at school to see the Nutcracker every winter. The kids at school were always put in a trance every year by the actors and actresses performance. Pam wished she'd never stopped teaching. She had many fine experiences teaching. The field trips were always the most fun. Pam got up to go in and take her medicine early. The nurse wanted to soak her toe, but they didn't have time. They drove downtown to the play. It was relaxing just to get away from the building for a while. Her understanding was that the play would be free. They drove up to the door and everyone got out of the van and went into the studio. They watched as they acted out about a couple who were having affairs behind each other's backs. The play was a comedy. Pam laughed until she couldn't laugh anymore. The play ended with the couple getting back together. On their way out of the studio Pam noticed people staring at them. They seemed offended they had come to the play. This almost ruined the whole trip for Pam. The patients didn't seem conscious that the guests there were looking at them. Pam felt a little ashamed and looked at her own clothes. They weren't dressed for a play. They all piled back into the van. Soon they arrived back at Grassy. Pam took her sleeping medicine and lay down. She said a short prayer.

Pam didn't go directly asleep. She tossed and turned until about one o'clock. Then she got up to ask the nurse for some Tylenol. Sometimes this helped her to go to sleep. She had to make up that something was hurting her before they would give her Tylenol. She told the nurse that her toe was hurting. Pam got two Tylenol and went to sleep.

Pam had only slept about four hours when she woke up the next morning. She felt on edge as she swung her legs over the side of the bed to go see what time it was. She crawled back into bed after finding out it was only six o'clock. Her legs wouldn't stay still. Pam's whole body was restless. She finally went back to sleep and slept until eight o'clock. She was making it a habit to miss breakfast. By the time lunch came around she was so hungry that she could eat almost anything. The morning had been busy. Her team leader approached her and asked if she would like to change rooms. She told him that she would. A desk and bed had to be moved into the new room. There were still three people a room. Her new roommates were nice to her. They talked to her and gave her the best spot in the room. "Lunch is now being served!" Pam could barely hear the intercom. She walked downstairs to the lunchroom. They were having meatloaf. She missed her two groups when she came back. She laid down in her new room to rest. While she was resting the therapist came in and told her it was time for therapy. She met with him and he wanted to know if she was worried about anything. She told him she wanted to go back to Jackson County to live. He said he could help her with this. Pam left his office to go to the telephone room. There she made a call to Comprehensive Care in Jackson County. She asked to speak to Sally. She wanted to check with Sally to see if they would place her in a family group home in Jackson County. She knew Sally because she had gone to Comprehensive Care before. Sally was busy so Pam told the receptionist to have her call her back if she could. Pam went to her room to await the telephone call. Pam hoped that Sally would be able to help her. She wanted a more country setting to live in. She wouldn't have to call Wade long distance if she lived with someone in Jackson County. Wade would be able to visit her more often if she lived at home. It was nearing four o'clock and Sally hadn't called her back. Pam decided to call her again. Sally was able to come to the telephone this time. She said that the family group home in Jackson County was filled up. She gave the number for social services in Jackson County. They might have a placement in a County that could be close to Jackson County. Pam thanked her and hung up the telephone. It seemed like there was no way Pam could be close to Wade.

It was getting time for dinner so Pam went in the library to wait. There were many patients there. Everyone was hungry and waiting to eat. Pam looked at the menu on her way up the hall. It didn't sound very good to her. They often had the same things over and over again. When she cooked for her family at home she had a variety of foods. She wished she could be at home to cook for her family again. The way it was she would never be back home again. Pam wasn't sure her sister would come and get her for Christmas. She hoped she would let her stay all night for Christmas. Pretty soon Pam heard them call for the patients to go down to dinner. Pam enjoyed the meal but wished they'd have sandwiches sometime. She'd eaten chicken until she thought she'd turn into a chicken. Pam came back upstairs to watch television in her room for a while. Then she went downstairs to smoke. There wasn't anyone in the smoke booth. She thought about Wade and how she hadn't talked to him since Saturday. She wished he would call her sometimes. It seemed like she had to do all the calling. It was hard to get phone cards. A thousand minutes didn't hardly last for a whole month. She was determined to make this phone card last the whole month. She went back to her room to journal. Pam tried to think back about what she did at home in her free time. She listened to the stereo, watched television, worked on learning centers for her classroom and talked with Wade. Here she had no stereo and the television only got three channels. She didn't teach any more to make learning centers. The situation at Grassy was hopeless. Maybe things would change but she doubted it.

After Pam wrote in her journal for an hour so it was time for a snack. She went to get her favorite soda diet root beer. They were out of root beer so she had to get diet coke. She drank the soda then went to take a shower and change into her pajamas. It wouldn't be too long until bedtime. She planned to lay down about nine-thirty. Pam was anxious for Friday to come. She was supposed to go to the foot doctor and have her toenail worked on. As she lay down she said a long prayer that night. She didn't know how quickly she would fall asleep. Pam just hoped it would be before one o'clock.

Pam woke up bright and early to find out that she was going to the foot doctor. The attendant was waiting to take her to the doctor. The doctor cut two ingrown toenails out. Pam would have to stay off her foot for most of the day. It was boring lying in bed all day. She watched two or three soap operas. One of them, Guiding Light, was her favorite. She used to watch Guiding Light as a teenager. The characters had changed but the story lines were similar to when she was young. Pam's toe hurt so she asked the nurse for some Tylenol. She gave her two tablets. Soon the pain began to wear off. It was like a toothache. The pain was a throbbing ache. She didn't have sharp pains but slow constant pain. Pam hoped her toe would be better tomorrow. This made twice she'd had to go to the doctor about it.

Pam slept much better in her new room last night. Her roommates slept instead of getting up and down all night. Pam was really becoming hungry. It wouldn't be much longer until time for dinner. She hadn't talked to Wade since last Saturday so she limped down the hallway to the telephone room. He answered the telephone saying, "Hello." Pam responded with, "How are you?" Wade said, "I'm resting. The golf is about to get me down." She replied, "I hope the gas prices aren't keeping you from driving to school." "Have you resorted to riding the bus?" Wade said, "Ronnie and I are taking turns driving back and forth." Pam asked, "Do you think the gas prices will keep you and daddy from coming to see me in three or four weeks?" Wade answered, "No. I'll always come to see you." Pam asked, "Are you liking your college course?" Wade replied, "It stinks. It's so boring sitting there." Pam told him many college classes were impersonal and boring to try to stick it out. They talked for a minute or two longer. Then Pam said, "I'll try and call you back Sunday. I love you." Wade said, "I love you too." With that the conversation was over. Now all she had to look forward to for the rest of the evening was dinner. The menu said stuffed cabbage rolls. The cabbage rolls weren't too bad. It was just what they had with them that made the meal not appetizing. White plain rice and carrot slices. Everything was unseasoned. It was impossible to eat their side dishes. It was hard to get filled up on just the main entrée. Pam waited for them to call dinner in the library. The intercom said,

"Dinner is now being served." She walked to the elevator and pushed the down button. The nurse had told her not to go down the stairs. She'd been using the elevator to go eat and to go outside. Pam was used to going up and down the stairs. It gave her some exercise. By the time she got downstairs to the dining room she had to be last in line. Her toe ached as she stood there watching the other patients get their food. She wondered what Wade was having for dinner. He had become so tall and slender. She bet he wasn't eating right. He was home alone every night while Harold visited his wife or went golfing. They were building a new house and planned to live together once the house was built. Why couldn't it be her instead of someone else? Pam asked herself this question over and over. She used to be sick all the time but now the new medicine she was taking was helping her. Pretty soon she would be able to live a normal life.

The table she sat at was full. Each person had to move a little when she sat down. She and Melvin sat and talked about going to Wal-Mart and Kentucky Fried Chicken. Pam still had to have someone help her ride the bus. It was too confusing for her to try to go on her own. Melvin said he would go with her to show her the way. Melvin was an old gray haired man. He used to drive a taxi in Lexington. He knew his way around town. He had lived at Grassy for about three years. His drinking problem had landed him where he was at. Grassy had a mixture of young and older people. Everyone had different problems. Some were mentally ill. Some had alcohol and drug issues. Others were physically handicapped. It was just supposed to be a two year program. Some of its patients had been there as long as eighteen years. Pam had the feeling that she would be there for a long time. Pam told Melvin she would see him later as she got up from the table. The smoking area seemed inviting so she headed in that direction. When she got there one of the supervisors was outside talking with the patients. It had rained earlier that day. Everyone thought it would be nice and cool. The air outside was hot and muggy. Everyone seemed to be sluggish sitting around while they smoked. Pam soon made her way back up to the activities room to her group Into the Garden. She wanted to see if her daisies had grown any taller. To her dismay they hadn't grown very much when she measured them. Pam liked the attendant who led the group. She was a short, thin brunette who talked very low.

She seemed very calming and shy. She let them participate instead of her doing all the talking. She discussed the main cash crops grown in Kentucky. They are corn and tobacco. Pam got her one hundred points for going to group. She went back to her room to journal for a while. It was stuffy in her room so she turned the air conditioner on low. She waited for it to be snack time as she wrote in her journal. Some days she didn't journal at all. While other days she wrote all day. Some days things seemed more interesting than others. The days that she didn't journal she wasn't having as many racing thoughts. Sometimes it was a mad rush to see if her fingers could write as quickly as the thoughts raced through her head.

The attendant wanted her to join the Fun and Games group at seven o'clock. She didn't want to stop writing but she decided to go ahead to the group. The group was fun. They played Bingo and she won a free soda. She was happy that she'd gone. Now she didn't have to spend her points. She took the soda outside to drink while she smoked. Debbie, one of the older patients sat beside her. They talked about how dark the clouds were. It looked as if it might rain any minute. Debbie said, "I love to look at the sky late in the evening. Don't you?" Pam told her there were many birds flying over. This was a sign that summer was coming to an end. Pam got up to throw her soda can into the recycling bin. She pushed the whole lid off the top of the can and it fell to the concrete. Pam hoped no one was watching. She felt a little guilty because sometimes she threw her can in the regular garbage. Pam knew deep down that it was silly to think someone watched which can she used to throw away her soda can. When she was really sick she thought people were watching and judging her every move. Who cared where she threw the can? She became so engrossed by the cans she didn't realize what she was doing. She had poured out the whole can of garbage onto the grass and began picking up every can she could find. She kept doing this until one of the patients ran over to her and asked what she was looking for. She stopped and looked up and said, "Cans." The patient then rushed into the building to return with an attendant. The attendant helped her pick up the trash and put it back into the can. Pam told her, "I was looking for more cans." The attendant saw that she was sorry and told her not to worry about it. Pam had felt guilty. In the meantime, she got lost in her thoughts about the cans.

The attendant told her not to worry things weren't that bad. She led Pam back into her room and talked to her for a little while. "It's not long before bedtime. Go ahead and take your medicine." Pam did as she was told. She really didn't understand what all the fuss was about. She changed clothes and took her medicine.

That night she prayed that she would see Wade soon and that he didn't find out about the incident with the cans. She prayed that tomorrow would be a new day and she wouldn't mess up again. In the back of her mind she wished she was at Saint James with all of her friends. Pam couldn't go to sleep. She tossed and turned all night. She got up twice and told the nurse her toe was hurting. The worse thing about the procedure was the three shots that she numbed the toe with. Pam couldn't tell how the toe looked because it was wrapped up in gauze and a bandage. Pam finally went to sleep sometime after one o'clock.

Pam didn't wake up until about eight that morning. She had missed breakfast again. The nurse came to her room about ten o'clock to get her so she could remove the bandage around her toe. As the nurse took the bandage off Pam felt pain. Tears came to her eyes as she sat there in disgust. The toe was all bloody. The sides of it were slightly open where the doctor had removed the ingrown nails. Pam began to soak her foot in Epsom Salt. The warm salt water first stung a little but then felt soothing to her toe. After she finished soaking the toe it felt much better without the bandage on it. It looked sickening but felt better.

Pam gathered herself up and went downstairs to the smoking area. She sat there and talked with Donna for some time. They talked about her foot and then about how thirsty cigarette smoke made them. Soon it was nearing time for lunch. They looked forward to the chicken salad and soup. Pam began thinking about the incident with the cans the night before. She got up to go back upstairs. Donna walked up the stairs with her. Donna was a clean looking older woman. She was around sixty-five years old. Pam wondered why she was in a place like this. She seemed so normal. Donna had said once that she was in a nursing home before she came to Grassy. Growing old scared Pam, she hoped she made it until she was sixty years old. Then she would have her full retirement and not have to fill out papers any longer. Pam and Donna made their way to the library to wait for lunch. There weren't too many people in there waiting today. If you waited in the library you could get down to the dining area much quicker. Pam had learned that the people who got there first get less on their plates though. She decided to lag behind the rest. She was especially hungry today. She went to bed hungry the night before. Her weight showed she wasn't starving.

It was Saturday and there wasn't much to keep a person occupied. There weren't any groups on Saturday or Sunday. Pam didn't feel like lying around or sleeping. So how would she occupy her time? She didn't have the money to go shopping. She didn't usually bath until bedtime. Taking a shower didn't take all day anyway. The doctor had told her to stay off of her foot for a couple days. She knew she would end up watching television for the biggest part of the day. She lay on her bed restless. She got up to go downstairs to smoke. Raymond was out there smoking. He'd asked her to go with him about three weeks ago. She couldn't stand the thoughts of his hands all over her. She told him that she was much too old for him. This seemed to satisfy him for the time being. When she walked closer to the table, she heard him yell, "Pam!" As if she was a dog or something. He began to talk to her. He asked, "Would you like to buy a set of headphones?" Pam said, "No. I don't listen to music very much. I don't have a radio or C.D. player." He always wanted something. If it wasn't a cigarette it was money. That was the way most of the patients were at Grassy. They acted as if she didn't have anything better to do with her money than give it to them. Pam became tired of the situation and went upstairs to buy a soda out of the Pepsi machine. This was the last seventy-five cents she had until Monday. She allowed herself fifty dollars a week to get by on. The rent wasn't as expensive at Grassy as it was at Saint James. She allowed herself a little extra money. Saint James work program usually made up for the amount of money she spent. Here she was worried about money again. She had so little. Why did she worry over it? She went back to her room to drink her caffeine free soda. Even though it was caffeine free she knew the sugar would make her restless too. She felt it wasn't really what she ate or drank but what her illness did to her. As a girl growing up she could remember restless nights of not being able to be still. She got up out of the bed. Then she never took any medicine. The restlessness began to subside when she became an adult. After she married she couldn't get enough sleep. Then after Wade was born her sleepless nights gradually got worse until she finally went months without sleep. Pam decided she'd been bipolar her whole life. She just didn't get really sick until her late thirties. She wished she hadn't got sick at all. Sometimes she thought Harold wanted rid of her anyway. He went for long periods without talking to her after Wade was born. She didn't have the slender figure that she once had. She wasn't fat after the baby was born but she wasn't extremely thin. He always wanted her to be super thin. He claimed she had a double chin and everything. She couldn't have a double chin. She only weighed about one hundred and twelve pounds after Wade was born. She was really heavy now. She weighed close to one hundred and fifty. She was also going to be fifty years old in December. She was around thirty-seven or thirty eight when she first noticed a difference in her feelings toward things. That was ten to twelve years ago. She has been sick for that long. Wade is now eighteen years old. She had about five or six good years with him.

Pam lay on her bed wondering what she could do for the rest of the evening. This was just a lazy Saturday. Most of the patients were sitting in the dayroom. She didn't want to sit with them for some reason. She had never been able to occupy her time with other people. Even when Pam was young she used to sit in the back of the class by herself. Pam remembered many things about school. Pam had a first grade teacher named Mrs. Johnson. Mrs. Johnson came to the back of the room yelling, "You'd better pay attention." Pam thought she was referring to her. She was yelling at the boy who sat in front of her. Mrs. Johnson kicked the desk that he was sitting in until he jumped up and crawled under Pam's desk. Pam began to scream when Mrs. Johnson began to kick at the little boy. She hit him with her foot on the back. She kicked Pam in the legs. Pam tried to get up and her seat turned over. Mrs. Johnson was in a rage. Pam ran down the hall to tell the principal. By the time she made it back with the principal the boy was laying behind his seat crying. All the children in that classroom were crying. The principal pulled Mrs. Johnson out of the room. Pam and her classmates could hear him asking her questions. "You are dismissed." They heard him say. Mrs. Johnson never returned the rest of the school year. Pam heard her uncle say that Mrs. Johnson had been fired. Pam's uncle was a board member with the Jackson County school system.

Once she was in the third grade class of Mrs. Rawlings. Pam met a boy in the class that she liked. His name was Alfred Murphy. Alfred gave Pam a birthstone ring for Christmas. He gave it to her at the Christmas party. Pam was delighted to get the ring. She had to take the ring back to school because she found out it was his mother's ring. Even though Pam couldn't wear the ring because it was too big she still loved it. That same year she caught walking pneumonia. She had to stay home from school for three weeks. There was a home bound teacher that came to her home each day. She didn't do much school work with Pam. Pam's aunt Freda and she mostly spent the time talking. Soon Pam was well enough to go back to Mrs. Rawlings' class. Mrs. Rawlings had missed Pam so badly that she moved her seat to the front of the room. Pam always said Mrs. Rawlings was her favorite teacher after that.

Pam began to love school in the fourth grade. She was in Mr. Hay's class. He always had her write stories then draw some illustrations to go along with her story. The stories and pictures hung in the hallway next to his door. People entering the room always stopped and looked at Pam's stories. She loved Mr. Hays for teaching her to read and write properly. Pam couldn't remember her fifth grade teacher. She had no idea who she had in the fifth grade. Pam remembered sixth grade because she had Mrs. Stevens. Mrs. Stevens always let Pam keep her daily attendance book. She would copy the names every six weeks in her book. Pam learned every name of each student in Mrs. Stevens' class very quickly. She also remembered being in that class because a boy named Bennie sat behind her. Bennie was always pulling Pam's hair or grabbing her butt with his hand. She began to get irritated at this because it happened almost every day. One day she slapped Bennie across the face. Mrs. Stevens took Pam out in the hallway and asked her why she did this. Pam told her what he had been doing to her each day. Mrs. Stevens changed their seats and told Bennie to stay away from Pam at recess. Pretty soon Pam had almost forgotten that Bennie was her classmate.

The seventh and eighth grade was the place where she learned how harsh teachers and parents can be. The seventh and eighth grades rotated rooms. The first thing that happened to her was she won to be a seventh and eighth grade cheerleader. The team tried desperately to find a cheerleading sponsor. They couldn't get any teacher to sponsor them. They ended up getting an aide to do the job. Their uniforms were supposed to come back black and gold but came back black and a dull yellow green color. The cheerleading squad the year before them won the trophy. How could they win anything? They got off to a bad start. Then Pam had an argument with her seventh grade teacher Mrs. Thomas. Mrs. Thomas kept giving her D's on her spelling work. Pam had always made A's in her spelling. Mrs. Thomas told her if she would get her mind off cheerleading that she might get decent grades in spelling.

Pam soon discovered boys. There was a high school boy who came over to her next door neighbors. Her neighbor was the boy's granddad. Pam finally found out the boy's name was Harold Combs. Little did she know that when she became a little older she would marry Harold. She always made sure he saw her riding her bike up and down the lane when he came to visit his granddad. When they began talking a little bit Pam was told to come into the house. She wasn't allowed to talk to boys until she was eighteen. This made life miserable for her. She tried to get involved with school but she couldn't concentrate. She wasn't even allowed to talk to her girlfriends over ten minutes at a time on the telephone. She had put Harold Combs in the back of her mind until she was a little older.

Finally, she passed to the eighth grade. The second week of school she got in trouble with Mrs. Williams for chewing gum in her history class. She was put out in the hallway. When she saw the principal Mr. Blevins walking up the hall she immediately went to the water fountain to get a drink. She pretended not to be in any trouble. Mr. Blevins later asked Mrs. Williams about it. Mrs. Williams told him the truth. Mr. Blevins pulled Pam out of her math class and took her to the office. There he gave her two licks with his paddle. She felt so embarrassed she had never had a paddling at school in her life. What would she tell Aunt Freda? She decided not to tell Aunt Freda anything. Later on in the school year her spelling teacher Mr. Carrier came to talk with her aunt and uncle. She heard him tell her uncle that she wasn't near the student Jenny her sister was. He told them that she was a little above average. Pam dreaded going in his class the rest of that school year.

How could he say such a thing? She had made A's too but had to study a little harder than Jenny. She passed the seventh and eighth grade but didn't receive any awards except in English.

She entered high school with a B average. Pam's first year in high school was embarrassing. She had to go to remedial reading and math. Pam's test scores were low in these two areas. Jenny was in accelerated classes while she was in a slow learner classes. It was about more than Pam could take as a freshman. Her sophomore year was much better. She was in regular classes carrying an A average. Pam was proud of her A average. She would walk up and down the hall and show everyone her report card. She was thankful that Jenny helped her study. She began taking business courses and did well in them. She had several boys interested in her and they had asked for her telephone number. She always made up some excuse why they couldn't call. She just couldn't bring herself to tell them the truth. By her junior year the boys had stopped asking. Word got around that she was too busy. Pretty soon she didn't get any dates at all.

During her senior year Pam took a creative writing class. Her teacher Mrs. Durham praised her work. Once she even showed her work to the staff with Pam's permission. She finally got to take Driver's Education the second semester. She turned eighteen in the middle of the school year. Pam felt happy because she was allowed to date and drive in the same year. It wasn't until summer that she spread her wings. Guess who asked her out? It was Harold Combs. He had a good teaching job and was interested in her. They began to date. Pam took summer school at E.K.U. and dated Harold at the same time. She found her courses in college to be easy. She hardly ever opened a book. She and Harold dated all summer. Then in early fall he just stopped calling her. She didn't know why. They had dated for four or five months. He must have met someone else. She was heart broken. She didn't call him because she'd been taught not to call men. She could hardly study for worrying about him. After several months she got over it and just got into her studies. She didn't date anyone else. There was a football player that she ate with in the grill every evening but they didn't date. Fall turned into winter and pretty soon it was almost Christmas. Pam broke over and wrote Harold a letter. He called her in January wanting to date again. They dated that spring, summer and fall. Then he asked

Pam to marry him through the winter. They set their wedding date for next fall. They were to marry on August the thirty-first. Pam had three years of college in by the end of two years. She had gone to summer school and intercessions. This put her up to three years of college. They married that fall. Money was tight so Pam had to quit college and go to work. Pam went to work just after their honeymoon. She got a job as a receptionist at a nursing home. She was to fill in for Michael's mother while she was on sick leave.

Pam and Harold's honeymoon was spent in Lexington. They stayed at the Hyatt Regency their first night. The second night they spent at the Ramada Inn. Harold was such a gentleman he made her feel pretty like she was pretty and special. She loved him more than anything. They returned to their little rental house in Berea. There they stayed for about one year. Pam only worked at the nursing home for about three months. She got a better job in a factory called Hyster in Berea. She worked in an office as a secretary. After about nine months she got laid off. Her special project she had been hired for was over.

Harold and she moved back to Jackson County where she got a job at the Central office as a migrant coordinator. They lived in her aunt and uncle's little farm house. They were so happy there. Pam had a cat named Samantha. She was like a baby to them. After about a year Pam quit her job at the Central office to go back to college and get her degree in education. It only took her two semesters. Then she was ready to teach by the fall. She didn't get a teaching job right off the bat. She had to wait until second semester to begin her teaching career. When she got her teaching job she was thrilled that she was going to teach in the same elementary school that Harold taught in. Money was tight so they drove to and from work together every day. They lived in that little farm house for about five years before they built a new brick home. The little farm house was four rooms with a bath. It was warm and cozy. They put down new carpet in it when they moved in.

Soon Pam and Harold were able to have two vehicles and a new house. The new house was about sixteen hundred square feet including the basement. They had three bedrooms and two bathrooms. They lived there about four years before Pam got pregnant with Wade. Each year on their anniversary they would go to Mammoth Cave. They did this up until the time Wade was born. They went to Mammoth Cave and Tennessee for their anniversary after this. Pam was so happy. She wished things had stayed this way. Then sickness struck and everything fell to pieces. Pam took the overdose of pills, after that the divorce happened. Pam thought everything would be alright. She should have realized that when Harold didn't remarry her that he wasn't serious about their relationship. He just came back until Wade got old enough to leave for good. Wade was fourteen years old when Harold left with him the second time. Pam was having a hard time facing the fact that she was in a period in her life where she might have to spend the rest of her life being sick. How could she cope with being confined? Grassy wasn't that bad, it was the situation that was hard for her to deal with. Her health and mental stability were failing her. Tomorrow would be Sunday. How would she spend another long day? Last Sunday she spent part of the evening with her sister. How would she get through this Sunday?

Chapter 12

Pam awoke and saw the nurse standing in front of her. She told the nurse that she didn't get to sleep until after two. The doctor had come and gone that morning without seeing Pam. The nurse said he read the notes that they had written about her sleep, but didn't say anything. Pretty soon Pam was going to fall over from exhaustion if the doctor didn't adjust her medicine. Pam asked the nurse if it were policy to let their patients go without sleep. The nurse didn't like this question. She changed the subject and told her to come and take her medicine and soak her foot.

Pam had missed her breakfast again today. She went outside for a while. The night air had been warm and muggy. There was a warm breeze blowing hard as she sat on the bench. Pam had told Wade that she would call him. He would be up around noon, she would call him then. There wasn't much going on outside so Pam waded through the gravel to the side door. She climbed the stairs to the second floor. She rarely became out of breathe going up the stairs. Her blood pressure had been up that morning so she climbed the stairs slowly. She knew that not sleeping wasn't good for her.

The building was hot and stuffy from the following day. The air conditioner at Grassy didn't work sufficiently and the building was hot. Many nights the patients lay awake sweating in their beds. They didn't even have fans for when the air conditioner didn't work. Even on the news it showed where elderly people got free air conditioners and fans.

There was supposed to be a new Grassy built sometime next year. Pam was looking forward to this. Maybe the air conditioner would be new and put out more cool air. Pam wanted to talk to the board about the living arrangements at the new Grassy, but every time she brought it up to the staff it seemed like they would just change the subject. How could she live in a place like this much longer? When would something good happen for Pam and the other patients at Grassy?

Pam returned from lunch around eleven fifty. She walked to the telephone room. There she placed a call to Wade. Harold answered the phone. "Hello, how are you?" Pam asked. Harold said, "I'm a little sleepy I stayed up all night at Tyner last night." She knew he meant he had stayed all night with his new wife. "When are you and Wade coming to see me?" asked Pam. "We'll be down in two or three weeks." Harold replied. "I hope I can come to Jackson County before to long." "How will we do that since you are married?" Pam said. Harold told her that he would let Wade show her around but he would come with him to pick her up and drop her off. Pam asked to talk to Wade. Harold said Wade was gone on a camping trip with some of his friends from school. He told her that Wade would be home around three o'clock. Pam said, "I'll call back later today." With that they said goodbye and hung up the phone. None of the family ever called her she had to do the calling most of the time. She wanted them to call her too. Pam left the phone room to have points taken off her notebook.

Pam walked to her room to gather up her cigarettes to go outside. There were quite a few people sitting around, but she didn't talk to any of them. She stared at her toe as she took puffs off of her cigarette. She wondered what Wade and his friends ate while they were camping. Jackson County was a good place to camp. There were all kinds of creeks and forest areas there. Pam liked camping as long as the weather was nice and there was a tent and a sleeping bag. She had been camping only three times in her life. She and Harold went camping at Tyner Lake one year. They went with Jenny and her husband. They fished and held hot dogs over a campfire. It was extremely hot the evening that they went camping. They lay in their tents that night while the sweat poured off their bodies.

When Pam was at Saint James she went on two camping trips. Both times she had a good time. The weather was about seventy two degrees and fair. They sat around the campfire and sang songs and told ghost stories. The stories were the best part because they could hear sticks breaking in the forest. They could hear things creeping and leaves rustling on the trees as they sat by the fire. The patients at Saint James had used their tokens to buy the camping trip. It was worth a hundred more dollars a month to get to go on trips. Saint James took them to the movies and bowling once a month too.

As a girl growing up Aunt Freda and Pam's uncle took them on cookouts all the time. She and Jenny would roast hot dogs and marshmallows over an open fire. They enjoyed pouring pails of water from the creek over the fire. They always made sure the fire was out before returning home. When they got ready to leave they got jugs of fresh spring water from Earl Johnson's spring. The fresh spring water always tasted natural. The summer was always enjoyable in Jackson County.

During the winter Pam and her sister would ride boxes on the old cliff behind their house. It was delightful to land in the powered snow. One day they got in trouble with Freda. The cliff became too slick to climb back up with their boots on. So they climbed up the side of the cliff in their bare feet. The snow was wet and cold as they climbed up the cliff. They didn't slip or slide back down the cliff with their shoes off. Aunt Freda saw them in their bare feet. She was trembling she was so mad. She told them to come back to the house and to break off two switches as they came. She told them that they would have pneumonia. They handed the switches to Freda. Inside the house down in the basement Freda swung the switches at the bottom of their legs. The switches didn't bring the blood but left red lines across the back of their legs. Pam and Jenny never talked about the whipping to anyone. That was the first time Freda had ever whipped either of them. Pam had her face slapped once or twice for sassing but never had been actually whipped. They knew better than to go barefoot in the snow.

Pam's thoughts about her adventures were running away with her. She wished she could calm down and go to sleep. Instead of taking a nap she went to the midday cafe. There were six people there counting her. They talked about the weather alert. They couldn't go outside during the alert. Jacob came in with some blueberry muffins. He gave each one of them a muffin to eat. The cafe served drinks but no snacks. It was hard to get anything extra to eat at Grassy. It was three meals a day or nothing. Pam hoped Wade would never have to live in a place like this. She got up to go back to her room. She would try and lie down to nap one more time. Pam hoped she would be able to leave her legs still. The nurse kept telling her that she would talk to the doctor about her racing thoughts and restlessness.

It was getting close to time for Pam to call Wade. She wondered if she should call him around three o'clock or wait until after dinner. She decided to call him later that evening. She was afraid that if he weren't at home that she would be using her points for nothing. It was Sunday; she always talked to him on Sunday. The afternoon was becoming long. She couldn't go outside because of the weather alert. She couldn't sleep because of her restless legs and her racing thoughts. She sat and held her head in her hands rubbing her eyes for a long time. She would rock back and forth on her bed. What was she going to do until dinner time? She just couldn't sit and stare like some of the other patients. Boredom was Pam's worst enemy. Pam flipped through the channels on her television. There wasn't a movie on. The day room didn't have their television on because it was quite time. She picked up her cigarette case and headed toward the other end of the hall. She would use this staircase to go outside and stand on the ramp. If she got caught she might be banned from smoking for a day or so. Why did Grassy mind for people going outside? It wasn't lighting or raining. There were people who had signed our earlier that were still gone. Things just didn't seem to make sense when it came to their rules.

Pam had moved six times in the last ten years. She couldn't find a place called home. She had moved twelve times over the last twenty eight years. Nothing had been settled since she started college. Her job with the Jackson County school system was the only thing besides her marriage that had lasted for very long. Harold and she were together for eighteen years. Her job with the school system lasted eighteen years. Pam was like a nomad wandering around in central and eastern Kentucky. The people at Grassy were unlike anybody she'd ever known. She wanted to be home with familiar faces. She knew how it felt to grow old alone because that was what she was doing. Only she had started her old age a little too early. Soon she feared that Wade would be too busy to visit her. Harold would enter his golden years with his new wife and be unable to come and see her. Jenny would go into retirement and not be able to come and see her as often either. She would then be all alone. Pam wanted to be with her family as she grew old. The more she thought about things the more nervous she became.

Pam decided to break down and call Wade a little earlier than she originally planned. He answered the phone in a deep voice, "Hello." Pam said, "You sound like you're in one piece. The camping trip must have been fun." He said, "We didn't do any fishing but ate roasted hot dogs." Pam's mouth began to water. She told him, "I love my hot dogs black." He said, "Hot dogs are pretty good any way that you roast them." "Wade, do you think you could come and get me one day and let me go to Jackson County?" "I'll try to be over in a couple of weeks. Maybe we can go to an Italian restaurant and eat." Pam said, "I would love to go to an Italian restaurant to eat. I love their salad and bread sticks." "The bread sticks that you swish around in melted garlic butter are especially delicious." Wade replied. Pam said, "I'll be calling you later in the week. I can't call too much because it costs too much." Wade answered telling her that he understood. With that Pam and Wade told each other that they loved one another, then gave big kisses over the phone and hung up. The conversation was a pleasant one. At least he was all in one piece from his camping trip.

Pam went and had twenty five points marked off her point book then she walked to the library to wait for dinner. They were serving turkey sandwiches, potato chips, cottage cheese and carrot sticks. This was just the kind of dinner that Pam liked. Sometimes sandwiches could be more filling than a meal where just meat was served as an entree. She put a note in the suggestion box about things she would like to see served at their meals more often. They had been having things that were hard to eat too often. When Pam got to the library Donna and Steven were sitting there reading. They put down their books to talk to her. They went over what Grassy was having for dinner. The intercom said, "Dinner is now being served." Everyone jumped up and ran to the downstairs door. They rushed as they went down the steps single file. Darlene yelled, "Everyone move out of my way!" No one listened to her. She yelled again, "You freaks get out of my way!" She was pretty upset that she didn't get to go first. Everyone was in line pushing and shoving to get to the front. The person behind Pam hit her in the back with the edge of his tray. She turned around and told Jessie to watch what he was doing. The person in front of her stepped back; and hit the end of her sore toe with his shoe. She was getting beat to death in line. She finally just went and sat down and waited for the line to die down. It was like this at every meal. It's a wonder that there weren't fights that broke out. The patients didn't fight but used much foul language. She believed they were used to getting by with foul mouths. Pam grew up in a household where you didn't use foul language. If you did you had to write that word one thousand times.

It was growing near bedtime and Pam hoped she could sleep. The night before was a disaster. She missed her breakfast and the doctor both that morning. She couldn't understand why the nurse didn't wake her and tell her to talk to the doctor about her sleeping patterns. What kind of doctor came to see his patients before breakfast anyway? Pam changed into her pajamas and did some relaxation techniques that she learned in one of her groups. Her medicine needed changing desperately. As she lay down on the bed she began to say the Lord's Prayer. Then she thanked him for her son Wade and the money to have food and shelter with.

Breakfast consisted of an egg, toast and cereal. Pam ate toast with butter and jelly on it. Then she returned to her room to brush her teeth. She was still sleepy from the night before. She lay down on her bed for a minute. The minute turned into an hour and a half; it was nine thirty before she got her medicine and did a.m. care. She missed a group also. She soaked her toe and then went back to her room. There weren't any more groups until noon. She decided to lie down until lunch. Monday's usually didn't have too many groups. It was going to be like Saturday and Sunday, a slow day.

The night before, had been a rough night. She got up about ten times to go to the bathroom. She snuck to light up a cigarette but then got scared and didn't light it. She didn't want to get kicked out of Grassy. Where would she go if she got kicked out? Her body and mind wouldn't let her sleep until about two in the morning. She wanted to sleep but couldn't relax.

It was time for group. The group consisted of about four people. Pam liked her 'This is Your Life Group.' It gave everyone a chance to reflect on their past life. Today they had to tell about an event in their life from eighteen years old to twenty years old. Pam told about when she was saved and baptized. She got saved in a car when she was eighteen years old. She and her best girlfriend were parked in front of Sandra's house. She and Sandra prayed to Jesus Christ. Pam told Jesus she believed in him. She cried as she nervously asked his forgiveness. There she accepted Christ as her savior. She felt a warmth come over her that she'd never felt before. Christ saved her at that moment. She had never felt such a feeling. She had a quickening feeling but only for a moment. It was a special embrace from God. A few weeks later Pam was baptized on the Ratcliff farm. She was led by the preacher of Kerby Knob Baptist Church to a small green colored pond. The water was clear and a light green shade. There she stepped into the clear water. At first the water was up to her knees, as they walked farther it surrounded her waist. Pam wore a black skirt, red blouse and white vest. Her feet sank into the muddy bottom of the pond. It was spring and the wind still had a chill to it. The water had a cold bitterness. Pam didn't mind. All she thought about was Jesus Christ. The preacher covered her mouth and nose with a handkerchief. He lay her quickly back into the cold water. She just remembered the peaceful feeling she had while underneath the water. When she stood up from the water she yelled in a faint voice, "Praise the Lord." This was an event she would carry with her until her death. She wanted everyone in the group to feel at peace as she told her story. Some of them told how they were saved. Pam left the group feeling a sense of wonderment and peace. She went back to her room and thanked God she was still alive. She had broken her vows twice when she took pills. Now she realized that Christ was trying to tell her she was safe and to live in peace. She wished Wade could experience the warm embrace of Christ. She was going to call him as soon as he got home from school.

Pam's thoughts were interrupted by the announcement that the finance officer was giving out money. She hurried up the hallway to stand in line for her fifty dollars. The line was so long she went into the library to read. She picked up a thick book about Bill Clinton's life. She had always admired Bill Clinton. She broke her Republican vote to vote for a Democrat once or twice. She only wished he hadn't let a woman bring him down. It was sort of like Adam and Eve, only he wasn't married to Eve. She wondered if Adam and Eve were married. Pam became so involved with reading about Bill Clinton that she almost missed out on getting her money. She was the third one up from the last person. She went in and got her money. She was going to have to quit smoking. Buying cigarettes kept her from getting other things that she needed. Pam walked downstairs with her money. She went outside to see if she could find someone to ride the bus to get her a box of chicken livers at Famous Recipe. No one volunteered to do this. She couldn't go herself because she didn't know the way. Looked like Rally's was the only place she could get anything to eat. She didn't want to walk out there either because of her sore toe. Pam sat there and pouted for a little while; then got up from the picnic table. She would have to settle for dinner at Grassy.

Pam didn't have another group until six o'clock. So she went back to her room to journal for a while. In her journal she wrote about the times when she and Jenny went out to eat with Aunt Freda. Aunt Freda always took them to Burger King every Sunday evening. Pam always ordered a hamburger with extra onions and ketchup. Jenny always ordered a plain hamburger. They were just like daylight and dark on their eating habits. You've always heard the saying, "You are what you eat." Maybe what Pam had always eaten had caused her to have mental illness. She couldn't figure out why two out of three sisters had mental illness. Rita and Pam had mental illness. They both had been in car accidents that lead to head injuries. Rita's injury caused her to lay in a coma for weeks. Pam's injury was just a slight concussion.

Pam was riding with a friend and her baby. Pam began soothing the crying baby. This distracted her mother who was driving. The mother hit some loose gravel in the road and lost control of the car. The car flew over an embankment and turned over. The mother was wearing a seatbelt but Pam and the baby weren't. The mother grabbed her bleeding baby and flagged down a car. She went off leaving Pam behind. Pam stumbled out of the car to walk to a gas station. There was blood on her face. She called her sister in-law to take her to the emergency room. There they found out she had a concussion. Later that night Pam got a call at home telling her the baby had died. She felt like the accident was her fault because she was holding the baby. The mother of the baby told her to take the baby out of the car seat so she did. Pam grieved for a long time over her friend's baby. She always felt like her first baby was taken because of the death of her friend's baby. Pam and her friend remained on good terms until Pam developed mental illness.

After Pam took her first overdose she lost many friends. Pam's mother was mentally ill. It ran in the family on her mother's side. Her dad was a war veteran and principal of an elementary school until he died of a stroke at age forty two. So heart disease also ran in the family. Pam had both. Pam was only two years old when he died. Her mother became mentally ill so she went to live with her aunt and uncle.

It was growing time for dinner. Pam took her medicine and went to find William. He was outside. She asked him if he would go and get her some cigarettes and food at Rally's. He agreed to go. When he came back with the cigarettes and food she was broke. She had only allowed herself twenty-five dollars for that week. Pam asked him if he wanted some of her fries. She sat and ate a double cheeseburger and fries. Rally's, sold their food cheaper because all they have is carry out they didn't have a dining room. It was hard for her to get by on sixteen hundred dollars a month. She tried to save a couple hundred for Wade's birthday and Christmas. This left her almost nothing for clothes. She couldn't even afford cigarettes and a hamburger once a week. By the time she paid Grassy for the rent she was broke. Pam was broke no matter where she lived. The other patients at Grassy were broke too.

Pam came in to find her roommate Kelly singing to music on her headphones. Pam was going to lie down and see if she could nap but Kelly's singing was too disturbing. She kept singing over and over the same things. Pam tossed and turned in the bed. She could hear someone down the hallway yelling. Then there was Cindy who didn't pick her feet up when she walked. She scooted her feet which made a sliding sound. She passed Pam's door a hundred times. She scooted by every minute. Pam turned the television on loud to try and drown out the noises. It didn't help so she switched the television off. She longed for silence. She couldn't rest or concentrate from all the activity around her. Pretty soon it would be time for her six o'clock group. She hoped it was interesting like the last group they had. Into The Garden was a fun group. She was sure she would need to water her daisies this time. They didn't water their plants the last time. She hoped they would be blooming by Memorial Day. She would take them and put them on the baby's grave. Jobie Benjamin Combs was born in 1989. Wade was born in 1990. There was a year difference in their ages. Pam hadn't got too many points for the last four or five days. She needed them to make phone calls. If you got up to so many points you could save them and trade them for money. Soon it was time for group. They had to illustrate or use magazines to make a garden of their choice. Of course Pam chose to make a garden of daisies. She used one magazine picture and drew the rest with markers. It was a lovely picture of different colored daisies. She didn't quite get finished with it so the group leader told her she could finish it the next time. This group lasted only thirty minutes. They needed at least an hour and a half to do their illustrations. It was like being in the fourth grade again.

When she went back to her room the nurse came in to talk to her. She told Pam that the doctor had increased her restless leg syndrome medicine. This should help her rest and not be so active in the bed. Pam was relieved, but she wasn't sure it would help. She believed her racing thoughts were causing her not to sleep. The nurse said it would probably take three or four nights for it to work. Pam took a total of eight different kinds of medicine for her health and mental illness. After the nurse left her roommate Mary kept asking Pam how her toe was. Pam told her that it was much better. Mary showed her two coats that were given to her by a friend. Pam had only two coats herself. She left behind good clothes in her apartment. She didn't know why. Now she needed the clothes. That's the way she was when she was sick. She didn't realize half of what she was doing.

Pam went into the bathroom to take her shower. The floor in the bathroom was extremely dirty around the edges. She showered off quickly because it was cold. When she came out of the shower Angie was standing in front of her. Pam became sick and started throwing up when she saw her. Angie had stool splattered all over the front and back of her shirt. The stench made Pam's stomach turn. She ran to the garbage can where she threw up over and over. The smell had caused her to gag. She went out into the dayroom and told one of the staff that Angie needed help in the bathroom. The attendant went directly into the bathroom. She came out of the room and went into Angie's room to get her some clean clothes. After Angie came out of the bathroom Pam went in to spray disinfectant everywhere. This covered up the smell. The attendant seemed sick for an hour or so after the ordeal. Pam went to her room to put away her dirty clothes. She lay down on the bed and began to thank God that she had enough mind about her to be sanitary. She prayed that she wouldn't catch anything from all the germs that were floating around. She prayed for Angie. She prayed to go back to Saint James.

Pam was awakened at eight o'clock by her team leader Cindy. Cindy wanted to talk to her about how she was fairing. Pam told her that she wished they could give her some kind of nerve medicine other than Vistril. The Vistril seemed not to work well for her because she was letting things bother her too much. Pam had tried therapy but talking about things didn't seem to keep her from worrying. Cindy told her to make a list of the things she felt needed changing and they would discuss them during staffing on Wednesday. After Cindy left Pam sat down and made a list. The list was four things. They were a medicine change, to go back to Saint James, to have Wade more money and to be on some kind of work program. After she made her list she walked up to the library to wait for her nine twenty Brainiacs group. It wasn't long before they called the group. She liked the Brainiacs group. The group tested their skills in math and memory recall. Today they worked on multiplication in math. Pam got all her problems correct. In word recall they had to remember the names of different animal words. She got sixteen out of twenty of these correct. The last activity was remembering pictures of things. Pam remembered nineteen out of twenty of them. She earned four hundred points for this group.

One of Pam's friends in Grassy talked about leaving as they sat and smoked. He said he was going to another facility. Before he left he gave her a copy of the road map to Lexington to help her get around. Pam didn't tell him she couldn't get around even with the map. The bus routes were too confusing. Pam had to switch buses right in the middle of a trip. Pam often was afraid she wouldn't make it back in time for dinner. She would ask some of the other patients to help her with traveling on the bus.

The day had passed quickly. It was almost time for dinner. They were having tuna sandwiches, potato chips and jello. Pam thought the tuna sandwiches were good so she ate all of her meal. The taco salad they'd had for lunch was spicy and had upset her stomach. She could remember preparing tacos and tuna salad for Wade and Harold. They both were very picky eaters. She often had a hard time planning out meals that they would like to eat. At dinner Pam sat beside a young woman named Ellen. Ellen had a brace on her arm and leg. She ate almost all of her food. Ellen often walked from side to side up the hallway. She scooted her foot and bounced her body up and down as her right foot hit her left foot. She would do this for hours each day. Her doctor must have told her to exercise her weak leg. Across from Pam sat a man named Alex. He had frizzy black hair and black eyes. He ate with his head down the whole time. He very rarely spoke. Pam asked him, "Do you want your jello?" He said, "I'm going to eat it in a minute." She said, "I thought Ellen might want some more." He said, "No, I want my jello." Pam told him that was alright she was just checking. He must have gotten angry because he got up and changed tables. Dinner was soon over. Pam took her tray over to the kitchen area. She walked back up the steps alone. She went directly down to the smoking area. Melvin was out there smoking. Pam asked, "How long have you been at Grassy?" He said, "I've been here about eighteen months." "How much longer are you going to stay?" Pam asked. He answered, "I'm going to stay for a while longer." Pam said, "I'm going to try and go back to Saint James." He asked, "How long were you there?" She told him she was there a little over three years. Pam grew tired of their conversation and went back inside to journal and wait for her group Fun and Games. Pam was sure that the group would go outside. It was cool outside from the hurricane Ike that hit Texas. It became windy and cool in Kentucky, but there weren't any significant storms that came from it.

Pam called her boyfriend at Saint James. He had left Saint James for a while then came back just before she left. They had been calling each other every three or four weeks. She called and gave him her number a couple of days after she arrived at Grassy. He was quite a bit younger than she. His charm and good looks made her become interested in him. Soon it was time for her Fun and Games group. She had got lost in her thoughts again and was just listening to her boyfriend talk. She hung up the phone and went to the activities room. The group went outside and played Frisbee. The patients were given four tries to get the Frisbee in the box. Pam won the game because she got the Frisbee in with just two tries. She earned fifty points for going to the group. Pam went to the store and bought a soda for one hundred points. She had sixteen thousand points left.

It was nearing time for Pam to go to bed. She changed clothes and put on her old rags that she called pajamas. Then she brushed her teeth.

She took her medicine and went outside to smoke before going to bed. There she talked with one of the men patients. He said he had taken hard drugs before he came to Grassy. It had taken him almost a year and half to get off of them but he didn't have the money to get his own place and leave. He said he was ready to start a new life. Pam felt sorry for him and gave him a cigarette. She lay down on her bed that night hoping that Wade would never try drugs. The doctor had increased her sleeping medicine too, so maybe she would rest better tonight. Last night she went to sleep a little quicker than she had been. Maybe tonight would be the same.

Pam got up early the next morning. She finally made it down to breakfast. She took her medicine earlier and was able to go to her group Good Morning Grassy. In that group they talked about hurricane Ike and Kentucky's basketball program. They discussed how Kentucky was building a new gym. When the group was over Pam went into the library to wait for the next group. The group Histories Mysteries was always a group she dreaded. The woman that led the group always read to them. Her reading skills were poor and her voice sounded as if she had to force her words. She was so matter a fact about things that it caused the patients to lose interest in what she was reading about. Pam often sat with her hands across her face. The group finally ended in about thirty minutes. She read about Atlantis and a wild animal that killed sheep. Atlantis was before Christ and the animal she read about was discovered in the last decade. It had been spotted in the United States. It sucked the blood of innocent sheep. The team leader showed them a drawing of what it was suppose to look like. She talked with an excited voice this time which made the topic more interesting.

Pam went down to the smokers' booth after the group. There she talked with Jean. Jean was an older woman who was also in the group Pam had just attended. They talked mostly about how the group was more interesting this time. Then they talked about one of the patients who wore a short skirt to group. Pam told Jean that Donna's skirt was so short that she couldn't look at her for fear of seeing her underwear. Donna's skirt was very offensive to other people. They got up from smoking to go inside and wait for lunch. They were supposed to have barbeque sandwiches, baked beans and coleslaw. Pam almost fell on her way down to lunch. She had on her house shoes because of her sore toe. Her right foot twisted around on the staircase. Carla the librarian attempted to catch her if she fell. Carl said breathlessly, "Are you alright?" Pam replied, "I've hurt my foot but I think I can walk on it." Carla said, "Do you want me to get someone?" Pam said, "No I think my foot will be alright." Pam's foot was hurting though; she hoped she hadn't damaged it. She took her house shoes off and put on her flip flops. She limped slightly as she walked.

Pam's team leader came and took her to staffing. The meeting with the doctor and nurses didn't go well. They didn't change Pam's medicine. She tried to explain to them how many medicines didn't work well for her. They wouldn't listen they just told her that the increase in her medicine would take a few days to work. She had been through this with them the month before and got the same answers.

Pam got directly up from the group and went to call Shelly at Saint James. She talked with the administrator Shelly. Shelly said she would do some checking and get back with her the next day. Pam was almost sure Saint James would take her back. Shelly told her that she loved her and missed her. This was music to Pam's ears. She hoped and prayed Shelly would send someone to get her. Pam didn't think her sister would drive her all the way back to Saint James. Pam's boyfriend was still there. Pam was anxious to see him again. Pam hung the phone up satisfied that she would be able to go to Saint James and finish her days there. The staff at Grassy seemed unyielding at times. They let the patients bother other patients. The staff even needled at the patients. They told them things not to do before it even happened. Everything had to be perfect. The patients at Grassy were only human. Pam was trying to go back to a place where they made you feel at home. It would be for the best.

Pam talked to Jenny on the phone about going back to Saint James. Jenny didn't want her to go back. She said that they let her leave when she wasn't ready. She, also, said it was much closer on the family to visit her at Grassy. Pam told her that the family hardly ever visited or called. Jenny told her to do what she wanted but they couldn't keep driving back and forth to Saint James. Pam was in a dilemma. She had already told Shelly that she wanted to move. What would she tell her now? Shelly might not believe her if she ever called again if she didn't go this time. Pam went to bed disturbed that night. She couldn't sleep even though the doctor had increased her medicine. She got up from the bed several times through the night. Then she asked for a PRN. After they gave her the PRN she went right to sleep.

Pam awoke to the sound of the attendant's voice telling her it was time for breakfast. Today was room care day. They had to change their sheets, dust, sweep and mop. She had all these things done by nine o'clock. She would get a level four on her room care for the day. She talked to her team leader about leaving Grassy. He said she would be better off if she stayed. She told him that she would probably stay. She wanted to talk to Shelly one more time before she decided. He said, "We can't make a referral because we don't think its' in your best interest." Pam said, "I think you have to have a referral before they'll accept you at Saint James." He told her that she wouldn't be able to leave without the referral. This made her angry because she was her own guardian. Pam began to worry; should she call Shelly back? She didn't know what to do.

Pam wasn't very hungry but she would wait for lunch anyway. She wished she'd gone down to breakfast instead of trying to talk to everyone about being moved to Saint James. Room care was beginning and it had to be done before lunch. Pam had already finished her room care that morning. The staff had a meeting with the patients before they could do their room care. They wanted the patients to stop bumming and to try to earn more points by doing chores. Pam still wished she could go back to Saint James. Grassy never really told her that they wouldn't let her go until today.

Pam was tired because she was in the room with an older woman who got up and turned the lights on at five o'clock every morning. Pam didn't appreciate this. Lights were to be out from nine at night until seven the next morning. Pam put a suggestion in the suggestion box that roommates should follow the rules when it came to the lights being turned off at certain times. Her roommate was cold so Pam grew cold back. She didn't like being treated poorly. She always treated her students at school with respect; why couldn't she be treated with respect too? Pam's thoughts were running away with her.

It was lunch time and Shelly hadn't called back. She might not call like she said she would. Pam wanted to talk to her some more. Pam went on down to lunch. She sat across from a woman named Darlene. Darlene never stopped talking as she ate. She talked continuously while she shoved food into her mouth. Pam was amazed at how fast she ate and talked at the same time. Pam was finished with her lunch pretty quickly. She took her tray to the window and went upstairs to lie down and wait for the group Brainiacs. When it was time for the group she limped slowly down the hallway. Her foot had begun to hurt. She still wished Shelly would call. During Brainiacs they worked on a crossword puzzle as a group. The puzzle was extremely hard. The group worked on it for about a half hour before they could complete it. This group reminded her of how she used to teach her students how to work a crossword puzzle. She started off by using their spelling words. This wasn't an easy task because she had to make up the crossword puzzles. Drawing the crossword took a couple of hours. Soon the group ended. Pam was glad to get two free sodas for her crossword puzzle.

She went back to her room to journal and wait for her visit with the therapist. The therapist was a student just getting out of college. He was young and about her height. He slicked back his hair with a few bangs sticking up. He had terribly long feet. She couldn't imagine what size shoes her wore. He acted as if he wanted to establish good rapport with her so she just let her thoughts and ideas flow. It wasn't long before he came to get her for their session that day. They got all settled in an office that had only two chairs. She sat in one and he sat in the other chair. She began that day by telling about the first episode she had when she thought she might be getting sick. She was washing dishes at the window in her kitchen. She wasn't alone. Wade was downstairs watching television. Harold was gone golfing. As she gazed out the window she thought Harold walked across the lawn. It looked like him. She only caught a glimpse of his body as he walked. She saw the back of his head with hair curled around the nape of his wet neck. It was a hot summer day. Pam quickly looked toward the driveway. His black Blazer was no where in sight. She knew at that moment she had only imagined he was there. She can clearly remember what she thought she saw. It was scary to her. Now that she looked back on it she believed their marriage was going bad then. She thought she may have internalized many things said between them that led up to this episode. She can only remember bits and pieces of things that happened after this. The therapist listened attentively. He called it some type of name but she didn't catch what it was. It really didn't matter to her. All that mattered to her was trying to make the best of what was left of her life. She told him that she would love to live at a personal care home and work at a part time job. He said he didn't know if they would let her live at Grassy and work at a part time job for any length of time. He said that would be something her primary would have to look into. They ended their session by discussing the job situation. Pam told him she would see him next Thursday and left.

Pam walked outside for a little while. It was a beautiful day. It was about seventy-five outside. The sun was shining brightly. There wasn't a cloud in the sky. There was a slight cool breeze blowing. She just sat down underneath the trees and watched the traffic pass by. At one time the traffic was her enemy. She thought the cars were stalking and following her. She realized now that was only her mind playing tricks on her. How would she ever pick up the pieces of her life and put them together to form some kind of unity? She knew the staff at Grassy could help her if she only would give them a chance. They had to get her sleeping habits worked out first. Pam was willing to work with them if they were willing to work with her. Maybe she could get a job close by. She was going to talk to her team leader and primary. She wanted a job. Pam walked back up the stairs.

Pam lay in her room thinking about a job. The old air conditioner rattled as the fan put out cold air. She got up from her bed to turn the air conditioner off. It was set on low but it felt as if it were on high. She went to her closet and pulled out a light weight jacket. Fall was just around the corner. It wouldn't be long until everyone would be wearing long sleeves. She didn't have very many long sleeved tops as she went through her dresser drawers. She had decided to go back to Goodwill the next week and try to find some more tops. The tops only cost two dollars and fifty cents. She could buy four tops with ten dollars. The bus ride would cost her two dollars. That would be twelve dollars all together. She would get someone to go with her to show her the way. Pretty soon she would know her way around alone. Pam decided that she wouldn't venture out too far without knowing exactly where she was going. She used to drive in Lexington by herself all the time. But since she'd been sick she got turned around easily. The Goodwill store was a real step down compared to shopping at McAlpins. Maybe if she worked later on she could afford some new clothes. Pam used to be a snappy dresser when she taught school. She wore tan and black together very often. When she taught school you could wear jeans with a nice shirt or blouse. Now you have to wear dress pants. School teachers that live alone don't make enough money to have both a good car and nice clothes. For the amount of education they have they should make more money. She hoped Wade would find a better paying job than teaching school. If he drove a truck he would make more money than if he taught. He was a straight A student. He never made a B in school. He deserved to have a good job.

Pam lay back down on her bed. She turned on the television for a little while. Oprah was on the television. Pam had always watched her program. As she watched television she waited for dinner. She decided to go and look on the menu to see what they were having. It was Salisbury steak, baked potato, and green vegetables. Pam liked the potato but not the rest of the meal. She wondered who would sit across from her at the dinner table. She went back to her room until the intercom said, "Dinner is now being served." She waited for about five minutes and then walked down the stairs to dinner. The line was long so she sat down at a table with her empty tray. Her mouth watered while she waited. She couldn't wait to put butter, sour cream, and ranch dressing over her baked potato. Baked potatoes were a real treat at Grassy since they had instant potatoes most of the time. Pam sat down next to Grace. Grace was a lady who used a walker to walk with. She weighed about one hundred and fifty pounds. She told Pam that Lithuim had made her gain weight. Pam sat and watched her eat. She ate only one food at a time until it was gone. Pam didn't eat like that. She took various bites out of different foods. Grace asked, "How is your foot?" Pam replied, "My foot is better than it was yesterday." Grace wanted to know if Pam wanted her roll. Pam told her she could have it. Grace said she was on a diet but she would take the roll. They talked back and forth for a while and then Pam told Grace she would see her later. Pam had eaten everything except for the roll.

Pam stopped at the front counter on her way to her room. The attendant told her that someone named Shelly had called she wasn't in her room so they took a message. Pam said they should have looked for her. They said if someone's not in their room that they just take messages. They said that the woman who called said she would call back the next day. Pam knew Shelly would call back but she decided to call Shelly later that day. Pam went to the phone room to call Wade. He didn't answer the phone so she believed he must be golfing. She would try back tomorrow evening. She wanted to see what he thought about her going back to Saint James. He would probably say that Grassy was closer and to stay there. She wanted him to come and see her no matter where she went.

It was nearing time for her shower. She gathered her things up and headed for the shower room. She used to take baths with Wade until he was one year old. Then she bathed him every night until her was eight years old. She used to call him "sweet peas" as she bathed him. He liked his little pet name. Wade was the most loving and understanding boy. He never talked back to her or tried to be defiant to her. Everyone that came into contact with him loved him. Pam returned from her shower to comb her hair. It was sticking up everywhere. She was letting it dry naturally. It was surprising how wavy and curly it was. It was looking much healthier since she stopped using the blow dryer on it. Her hair was thick and mingled with gray. She put her things away. The dirty clothes went in the hamper while the brushes and shampoo went on the desk. She was satisfied that she might be leaving. She wasn't sure now that she wanted to go. There were people at Grassy that might be willing to help her get a job. Even though they were rude sometimes how could she pass the opportunity to get a job? It would fill up her day with something to do. Pam folded her blanket back and turned her sheet down to get ready for bed. She didn't have the chance to call Shelly or Wade back. She left the room to get her night medicine which consisted of a pill for psychosis, one for nervousness, two for cholesterol, one for restless leg syndrome and one for sleep. She washed down the pills with a cup of water. As she walked back to her room she prayed that she would make the right decision wherever she stayed. She asked the Lord to guide her in her decision.

Chapter 13

The words, "I can't help you," raced through Pam's head. Pam lay awake in her bed. She could almost hear Harold say, "I can't help you." He told her this with tears in his eyes when he wanted a divorce. She didn't need any help just love and understanding. He acted as though she was an animal that needed discarding. She only needed a little help with her doctor's appointments and medicine. He never went to one doctor's appointment with her. Even when Wade was sick Harold was always too busy to go. She'd always made excuses for him, but not now. It wasn't a thing that he couldn't help. It was a thing that he didn't want to help. He didn't love her. He loved someone else for a long time. Pam didn't think he even recognized his love for someone else. She didn't know if it was the woman he was married to now or not. All Pam knew was his love and support died a long time before she became sick. He was never around long enough to help her and Wade. Pam just hoped he would continue to come and see her with Wade. Wade didn't know the way and couldn't come alone. Harold wasn't a bad guy but when it came to her and Wade his expectations were so high that you could never satisfy him. She hoped he would figure this out before it was too late for Wade.

Pam crawled out of the bed to go call Harold. Wade answered the telephone saying, "Hello?" His voice was deep and sounded sleepy. "Well, you must have just gotten up." Pam said. Wade said he didn't have a class until nine o'clock. Pam asked him what he thought about her going back to Saint James. He said he thought it was alright but he couldn't come to see her as often. She told him that she wasn't sure that she would be leaving. She asked if Harold was around. He told her that he had already left to go substitute teach. Pam said, "I'll call back later this evening after he comes home." Wade said, "I love you." Pam said, "I love you too. Give me a big kiss." With that they hung up. Pam would make sure that she talked to Wade again this evening. He was too sleepy to talk this morning.

She headed to the finance officer's office. She wanted to tell him about the letter she had received in the mail. It was about her account. The way the letter read it meant that she may have two accounts. Pam was supposed to have only one account. Randy let her call the bank. They told her that the new address change meant that she had a change in her account. They reassured her that she didn't have two accounts. Pam was relieved she thought someone may be trying to get into her account. She also talked to Randy about getting a part time job. He said he would help her work towards getting a job. Pam couldn't get one at Saint James any more because they had to drop their work program. Pam had just about decided that she wanted to stay at Grassy. She wanted to work and make some money on the side. She would talk to Laura the administrator about work and the rudeness of her employees. Maybe things would change and she would like it better at Grassy.

It wasn't too long until her ten o'clock Histories Mysteries group met. She would be glad when that group ended. She had other things to think about. In the group they listened to the attendant read about the Lockness Monster, Mothman and Aliens. The group was more interesting today because they had a different attendant. He was filling in for the old attendant. The pictures he passed around were pictures that Pam had seen on television before. She said, "It's funny how when one person reads something it sounds so boring. A different person can make the same thing seem so interesting." The attendant laughed and said, "I'm just the very best." His voice was deep and interesting to listen to. Pam left the group to go back to her room and wait for lunch. It would be just thirty minutes until time for lunch. They were supposed to have cheeseburgers today. The side dishes were French fries and tossed salad. Pam was hungry because she'd missed breakfast again. Her roommate got up and turned the light on again at four-thirty a.m. Pam was getting tired of being awakened so early in the morning. How could Pam tell her that she was disturbing her without making her roommate angry? Pam saw a chance to tell her roommate. She asked, "Would you mind turning the light off after you leave our room during the morning? You are keeping me awake with it." Her roommate was really nice. She said, "I forget to turn the light off after I get up in the mornings." She didn't act mad at all.

Pam went to the telephone room to call Shelly. The call went through. Pam asked, "Is Shelly in her office?" The secretary answered, "She's not in her office at the moment. Can I take a message?" Pam said, "Tell her Pam Combs called and that she'll call back when she gets a chance." The secretary said, "Yes, I'll tell her." When Pam came out of the phone room it was time for lunch. She went downstairs to eat. The line wasn't too long. She sat down at the table across from Brad. He was bad to bum cigarettes off everyone. He never had cigarettes of his own. Pam noticed how messy he was eating. He let the ketchup from his hamburger drip on his fingers and shirt. He got up from the table like this. He didn't bother to use a napkin. Pam could hardly finish her lunch because her stomach began to turn at the very sight of him. His hair looked as though it hadn't been washed for weeks. Pam finished her jello and got up from the table to walk back upstairs. Lunch had been a bad experience for her. Many of the patients at Grassy didn't care about their personal appearance. She lay down on her bed to take a short nap. She wondered what Wade was having for lunch. She always paid his baby sitters extra for his food; plus took food for his meals. They always said he ate well. Wade really slimmed down when he became an adolescent. He was never obese but was stocky built. She always had trouble getting shoes and pants wide enough to fit him. Pam was deep in her thoughts when the attendant told her that she had a telephone call. Pam answered the telephone. "Hello." She said. "Hello Pam this is Shelly." "I talked to Brenda on the board and she said we would take you back as soon as there was a bed open." Pam said, "Go ahead and put me on the waiting list. I keep thinking about Saint James. I guess I'll have to come back as soon as possible." Shelly told her that she would. With that they said goodbye. Pam hoped that she had made the right decision. She was poor at making decisions. She should have never left Saint James to begin with. She might still be working if she hadn't tried to get out on her own.

Pam couldn't go to sleep so she went downstairs. She sat and talked to Eric. He was also trying to leave. He said, "I ought to know something within the next week." He saw Rhonda one of the staff members come out the side door. He commented, "That's a real bitch." "I've had to tell her not to talk down to me three or four times." Pam said, "She's not done anything to me. Shelia's the one I have trouble with." Pam tried to change the subject. It bothered her for someone to use profanity. Pam just kept thinking about being on the waiting list to Saint James. She hoped they would call her back before too long. One of her friends at Grassy was also leaving in the next couple weeks. The roommate she'd had earlier that threatened to kill her had left too. They sent her to another facility.

Pam couldn't wait to talk to Wade again this evening. She could remember calling him at the baby sitters. He was so small and sweet. He always called her "Pam" over the telephone. He had yet to call her mommy. Wade had spent most of his life listening to her over the telephone. The calls now were long distance and much more expensive. She only tried to talk to him once or twice a week. Unless she got a job she wouldn't be able to call him but once a week. It came over the intercom that the group Into the Garden was starting. Pam went to group. Group wasn't very long so she returned to take her four o'clock medicine. Then she went outside to join the smokers. It was cloudy outside. The sun peeked through the clouds about every fifteen minutes. Pam looked at the sky to see if she could see any cloud formations of things like animals and peoples faces. She didn't spot anything. George kept talking about dinner and how we were having fish. Pam said, "I ate so much for lunch that I'm not very hungry." George replied, "We wait so long between meals that I grow weak from hunger." Pam said, "I can see where the men would get hungrier than the women." She got up from the table and went back indoors. Pam wondered if Wade ever went hungry. She knew he enjoyed eating. He was a picky eater but always liked to eat the foods that he loved. She bet he would love to have her roast with carrots, potatoes, onions and celery around it. She would like to have that herself.

Pam thought Wade was lucky he had never been exposed to any physical or sexual abuse. He was raised by his parents. Pam wasn't so lucky. Her mom physically abused her when she was small. She chased her into the bathroom. If she caught her before she made it to the bathroom her mom would strike her on the legs and back. Pam and her sisters would manage to lock the door to the bathroom to keep her out. They would huddle up into a ball to feel each others safety.

Pam went to live with her aunt and visited with her granny. Pam was at her granny's one week while her cousin Wendell was there. Pam was only about four years old and Wendell was around twelve or thirteen. He would take her behind the shed at her granny's house. There he would pull down her pants and fondle her. He would then pull down his pants and rub his body against her. Pam felt like a tiny stone. She would turn her whole body into a stone. Wendell seemed like a giant centipede grabbing at her every move. If she could only crush his huge body with her small stone one. One day her granny caught him doing this. She sent Wendell away and Pam never saw him again. She couldn't remember his face but could always remember parts of his body and pieces of his clothes. Pam was glad that Wade didn't have to go through things like this. She got up to call him. He seemed so far away from her. She had cautioned Wade since he could walk about the dangers of others. She explained to him what to do if he were confronted with individuals that would molest or harm him in a sexual manner. She didn't know what sexual abuse was until she was older. Her granny and aunt discussed it with her.

Pam dialed his number and the call went through. It gave a busy signal. She would have to call him back later. She always hated it if she couldn't reach him.

Pam awaited her Positive Thinking group. She had to think positive about getting a job. She called her boyfriend at Saint James. He said he was outside smoking. She told him about how he could get a job at Grassy and take the bus back and forth to work. She told him it would be much closer for his parents to visit him. He said he would think it over; that he might come to Grassy to live. He said he was like her; that he missed her. One place was just as good as another to live. She hoped he was telling her the truth. Pam's roommate kept going in and out of the phone room while she waited for Pam to get off the telephone. Pam turned around and called Wade again. The line was still busy. She decided to wait until eight thirty and call him again. Her Positive Thinking group would meet around seven o'clock. She would ask the group leader more about getting a job.

Soon it was time for group. They discussed having a place to live and a place to get food. The group leader said that they might not like it at Grassy. She said there were many worse places. Pam mentioned the job program to her and she said that the administrators and supervisors could help her with it. She was one of the nicer employees there. The group told her how rude some of the staff were to its patients. She said she knew they were rude but sometimes people had bad days. Pam said she had complained about several of the employees too but they were still there and just as rude as ever. She told Pam not to worry about it that she would bring it up to the supervisor. Pam felt better after the class. She went to her room to get her cigarettes and free soda stamp. It was time for snacks. You got a free snack but had to buy your soda with points or a free soda stamp. The evening had flown by. Pretty soon it would be time for bed. After Pam had her snack and soda she called Wade. He answered the telephone this time. Pam told him about what Saint James had told her. He was glad and said he thought she would like it better at Grassy after she got some sort of job. She agreed with him. She asked him what he ate for dinner. He said it had eaten ham sent by Harold's wife. Pam was glad that he had a meal instead of sandwiches. She told him he needed an after school job. He said he was going to look for one after Christmas. They talked for a little longer and then hung up. Pam took her shower and got ready for bed. As she lay down she prayed that things would work out for her and Wade in the job situation. Her bed was especially hard this evening. She got up and turned her mattress over to see if it was more comfortable on the other side.

Pam was startled by the hand touching her. She sat up in the bed and asked, "What's wrong?" Her roommate said, "Do you remember you told me to wake you up for breakfast?" Pam quickly said, "Oh, I forgot. I believe I'll sleep a little longer. I'm still tired." Her roommate said that everything was alright and she would talk with her later. Pam lay in bed half asleep dreaming. She was dreaming that she still lived in a house in Jackson County. Harold came over to mow her yard. She kept taking him water to drink. The ground was dry and the grass crumbled under her feet. The only thing that needed mowing was the dandelions in her yard. In the dream she could always see his slender tan arms but not his clothing or body. She just kept bringing him water over and over. She finally woke up enough to realize that it was just a dream. She staggered half awake to the bathroom. The stench from the commode made her gag and throw up. Grassy needed to work on being more sanitary.

Pam went back to her room and changed out of her pajamas into jeans and a t-shirt. She had missed breakfast so she did her a.m. care and went to get her points written down. While she was at the counter the nurse came out and asked, "Do you want to take your medicine now?" Pam answered, "I think I'd better take it before it gets too late." Many of the patients refused their medicine then they would get sick and start arguing with the staff. They would end up in the psychiatric hospital because they were so hard to get along with. Pam sure didn't want to have to go to the hospital. After taking her medicine she went and got her pan to soak her toe in. The nurse gave her some Epsom Salt to soak it. After Pam finished soaking her toe the nurse poured a solution over it that sanitized it. Then Pam spread antibiotic cream over the surface of her toe. She was ready to go outside to listen to music and smoke. When she got outside the table was full up so she went into the smokers' booth. As she sat there she stared at the pavement in front of her. It was covered with ashes and cigarette butts. She wondered when it would be her turn to clean up. Jack kept pacing back and forth in front of her. He had his hands clasped tightly behind his back as if he were an army sergeant. He kept mumbling profanity under his breath. Back and forth he paced. Pam said out loud, "I wonder when Jenny will call or be over to visit?" It had been two weeks since her visit. Pam realized it would be weeks or months before she would call her. Pam didn't know if she should break over and call Jenny. Jenny had so much more money to call while Pam hardly had anything. She decided to wait a couple more weeks to see if Jenny would call. Pam left the smokers' booth and went in to the solitude of her room.

She lay down on her bed. As she lay there someone out in the hallway began using the vacuum cleaner on the piece of carpet that was in front of the side door. She couldn't concentrate. The noise seemed as if it were getting louder and closer to her. She got up from her bed and slammed the door as loudly as she could. She went back and lay down in a ball shape. Her knees were tucked under her chest. Soon she aroused herself enough to start journaling. She had gotten used to Grassy and there wasn't much to journal about. Things didn't seem to remind her of the past. She remembered things about Harold and Wade but not other things to journal about. Her teaching career seemed like a dream that she had. It didn't seem like she had ever been in the classroom. She spent years studying to teach and actually teaching. It was a shame that she couldn't remember any of it. It was like she'd gone through the motions without really knowing what she did. Pam's classes always had high test scores so she must have taught the right things. She won a Campbellsville College award in nineteen ninety-three. It was for excellence in teaching. Look what she had come down to now? She felt as if she were nothing. Just someone her family had to put up with. Pretty soon they wouldn't visit at all. Pam became so engrossed with her thoughts that it was almost dinner time. She quickly jumped up from her bed to run down the tiled hallway to the stairs. At dinner she sat with her roommate and another older woman. Both of them had peanut butter and jelly sandwiches. They didn't like the beef stir fry they were having. Pam ate the stir fry. It wasn't too filling because it only had a few chunks of beef in it.

Pam thought about Jenny. She couldn't wait for her to call so she decided to call her this evening. Pam needed to know about her mail and things. Pam got up and took her tray to the kitchen. She walked back upstairs to the phone room. There she dialed Jenny's number. The phone rang six or seven times. Jenny's voice came over the answering machine. It said, "Hello we're not here right now. Leave a message after the beep." Pam answered saying, "This is Pam. I thought I would call and check on the mail and see how you all are. Please call me back." Pam hung up the phone knowing that Jenny wouldn't return her call. Pam always had to do the calling. They didn't understand she was having a hard time buying telephone cards.

Pam grew tired of being inside so she went out to the smoking area again. Everyone was gathered around the table. Melvin asked her if she wanted to go to the yard-sale with him. She told him she didn't have the money. He said, "You can just go look around." She answered back, "I don't have enough money to ride the bus." He seemed to understand then. Pam didn't like being so poor. She had never considered herself poor until she got into Saint James and Grassy. The men in the group got up and began practicing karate. One of the attendants yelled out the door and told them not to be horse playing around; that someone would get hurt. One of the men yelled back at her, "You wretch!" She told them she would take their smoking privileges if they didn't stop. Pam wanted them to stop because they were bumping into people on purpose. She got up and moved to the smoke booth. One of the men sneered at her and said, "Who do you think you are?" Pam didn't say anything back. The weather outside was perfect. It was about seventy-eight degrees. The sun was shining and there was a slight breeze. Everything was green from the rainy days before. In just one week it would be the end of summer. Pam hoped that summer would linger on a little while. She wasn't a cold weather person. The cold air brought a chill to her body that couldn't be shaken until the next summer.

She would like to talk to Harold but didn't dare call his cell phone. He's probably at his new wife's house. Pam wondered if his new wife would answer the telephone and let her talk to Harold and Wade. She might just say, "I'll take a message." Pam may never be able to reach them once they move. Not one time during her illness was she unable to reach Jenny or Harold. She shouldn't be worried about reaching them. Pam looked around outside and walked around the grounds. There were many buildings there. They were on the same grounds as the psychiatric hospital. There was a gym for activities and a greenhouse to work in. They only let patients work in the greenhouse a couple hours a week. If Pam couldn't get a job out in the community she might be able to work at the greenhouse.

The traffic had picked up on the road nearby. It was Saturday evening and people were out doing things. She walked back into the building and went to her room. It wasn't five minutes before the attendant came and told her she had a phone call. She answered, "Hello." It was Jenny calling her back. She was wrong. Jenny did care about her. "How have you been?" Jenny asked. "I've been good except for my sore toe." "What's wrong with your toe?" Jenny asked. Pam said, "I had two in grown toenails removed." "That sounds painful." Jenny said. They went on talking and Jenny told her she had a refund on her telephone bill of seventy five dollars. Pam asked her to look up the number for the steakhouse she worked at on the computer. Pam wanted to call the two managers there who owed her money. Jenny gave her the number. She, also, wanted to leave Jenny's address so she would get her tax return from them. They owed her quite a bit of money. She shouldn't have loaned either one of them a cent. They shouldn't have asked an employee for money. Jenny and she told each other they loved one another and hung up. Pam tried to call the steakhouse. The line was busy. She called back in fifteen minutes and got Nathan the night manager. She told him she wanted her pay check and the money that he and Laura owed her. He said he could send her pay check to her sister's address, and he would try to get the money that was owed to her. He said he would mail out the money and the check together. Pam deep down was sure she would never see the money. She left the phone room to go to her room to change clothes. It was time for bed. She hadn't thought about her suicide attempts until she talked with Jenny on the phone. Jenny told her that she was safe at Grassy and couldn't kill herself there. Pam didn't say anything back; she just changed the subject. She didn't say what she was thinking to Jenny. It might scare her. Pam would talk to her therapist and tell him how worthless she had been feeling. In the past when she felt this way she would resort to taking pills to make the thoughts stop or go away. Pam didn't want to do anything to hurt the people she loved any more. She never really planned to take pills it just happened. As Pam lay on her bed, she prayed that Harold, Wade, Jenny, Jason and her brother in-law were safe. She thanked the Lord for every moment she was alive. She asked him for his forgiveness and to take away any suicidal thoughts she might have.

It was Sunday morning. Pam woke up to the sound of music in her head. The songs words sang, "Everything is happening. You're what I need." She turned over and tears trickled down her face. Of course she was thinking about Wade. She woke up to a song that brought sadness to her. She wanted to go and call Wade but it was too early. It was eight-thirty in the morning. It was time for her to get up and take her medicine. Before too long the words from the song faded away. She clearly wasn't happy. Nothing could replace a son or daughter. She wept silently for a while and then dragged herself out of the bed. She let her pajamas drop to the floor as she reached for her clothes. She didn't bother to pull the curtain. She stood naked next to her bed. Her roommates were already out of the bed and gone to the dayroom. They had been extra quiet this morning. She pulled her blue jeans on; then a black basketball shirt. She reached for her flip-flops. She couldn't wear shoes because of her sore toe. She gathered up her cigarettes and went outside to smoke.

The air was cool as she opened the side door to step out. It seemed to hit her face as cold water would. She was fully awake now. There wasn't anyone outside at this point. She sat down in a chair near one of the tables. She didn't light up her cigarette but stared at the ground covered with ants. She picked up a stick and began swirling it around to mess up the little ant hills that were built. Soon the ants began scrambling around trying to find the doorways to their home. Pam felt a little sorry for them and wished she hadn't disrupted their lives. She sat back and lit her cigarette. The cars and trucks passed quickly. It wasn't time for church yet. Why was the traffic so heavy? She wished she was at her home in Jackson County. She wanted to be sitting in her screen porch watching the traffic. It seemed like ages since she had sat there. She gazed at the vehicles as they spun by. She grew tired and walked back toward Grassy. She was careful not to step on the cracks of the sidewalk. She said a little saying out loud as she did this. "Step on a crack, you'll break your grandma's back." She kept saying this over and over as she skipped over the cracks. Her classroom used to do this as they walked around the building after lunch. Her kids at school loved to take walks after their meal. She enjoyed them too until the weather turned bitterly cold.

The phone rang several times before anyone answered. "Hello." Harold's deep rough voice rang through her ears. "How are you?" "I'm doing well." "Are you ok?" Pam said, "I'm awfully lonely. I wish I were in Jackson County." Harold asked, "Are you going back to Saint James?" "Wade said you might be going back there." Pam answered, "I'm on the waiting list." "Shelly thought by the time I got in that I'd be adjusted here and would want to stay." Harold replied, "You don't want to go back up that hallow." Pam said, "I can't ride the bus here without getting turned around. Saint James takes you to the store." "Well I'd rather be in Lexington than Hazard." Pam said, "We'll just have to wait and see how I'm feeling when it comes time." They talked about when Wade would be able to come and see her. Harold said Wade was still in the bed; that Jason had stayed all night. Pam told him she would call back later. She said it was getting hard for her to afford phone cards. Harold said Jenny and he would buy her a phone card if she needed one. Pam asked how they would know when she needed one since they never did call. Harold said they would figure it out when she didn't call them. Pam wanted to know when they would be over. Harold told her in a couple of weeks. He was nice to her on the phone. He said that he would probably be moving in his new house in about a month. "Wade will like your new home. I'll be glad when you move." Pam meant every word that she told him. She said, "Well take care. I'll talk to you later. Remember that I love you." She hung up the phone quietly and walked down to lunch. She was the last person in line. Pam sat by herself and ate. She thought of Harold and how much she really did love him. Harold and she had been through so much together why couldn't things have worked out between them? She sat and thought about this while she ate.

Pam let the phone keep ringing. Finally on the fifth ring Wade answered, "Hello it's me Pam. What are you doing?" she asked. "I'm just sitting around enjoying the weather." "Did Jason finally leave?" Wade replied, "He left a long time ago." "I wish I were there sitting around with you." she said. Wade sat a moment without saying anything back. Then he said, "I wish you were here too?" Pam said, "I'm really sorry that I got sick." Wade said, "Now don't talk like that. You couldn't help the way things turned out." Pam replied, "I guess I have to live somewhere." "Just remember Mommy that I love you." Tears came to Pam's eyes when he told her that. He very rarely called her mommy. "I'd better get off the phone now. I'll call you around Wednesday or Thursday." Wade said, "Call me later on in the week. The golf season will be over by then. Remember I love you." "I love you back." Pam said. "Give me a big kiss." With that they hung up. Pam couldn't wait to see his face and hands. When she would see them uncovered she could tell if he had grown. Things had somehow come to a standstill but were not completely over. Soon she would be able to kiss and hug him and tell him how much she loved him in person.

Pam had faith that things would get better. Many of the people at Grassy Personal Care Home would make everything alright. Pam felt as though God and her inner peace had to make reality more enjoyable for her to be happy. Soon she would learn to relish life and the simple things again.